LOTUS SEEDS

MARCIA BROWN

LOTUS SEEDS

Children, Pictures, and Books

CHARLES SCRIBNER'S SONS

NEW YORK

Copyright © 1949, 1955, 1962, 1967, 1968, 1972,
1974, 1977, 1982, 1983, 1984, 1986 Marcia Brown

Library of Congress Cataloging-in-Publication Data
Brown, Marcia.   Lotus seeds.
   1. Brown, Marcia.   2. Illustrators—United States—
Biography.   3. Illustrated books, Children's—
United States—Themes, motives.   I. Title.
NC975.5.B74A2   1985   741.64'2'0924 [B]   85-40288
ISBN 0-684-18490-7

1 3 5 7 9 11 13 15 17 19   H/C   20 18 16 14 12 10 8 6 4 2

Printed in the United States of America.

CONTENTS

PREFACE

The pond is full of Chinese lotus, great creamy white cups and huge leaves that are changing constantly, flopping this way and that in every breeze. The leaves are most interesting when they are nearing the ends of their lives. Torn by winds, battered by autumn rains, brown and ragged, they curl and droop over the seedpods until the seeds slip back into the mire to store up strength for next summer's blooming of that startling beauty and purity. One can understand why Oriental civilizations revered the lotus as a symbol of spiritual power and rebirth.

The ideas and images gathered by children from their books are like lotus seeds, endlessly reborn to bloom in successive seasons of their lives.

All one's life one learns from the lotus.

Marcia Brown

WHAT IS A DISTINGUISHED PICTURE BOOK?

"The picture in the mind is what counts. The elements that make it—gesture, movement, color, symbolism— all reinforce the same elements in the telling."

What is a distinguished picture book? With the changes that have come about in publishing in the last few years, the fate of the picture book lies squarely in the hands of librarians. Today it takes real courage for a publisher to produce a picture book, especially one that is a little unusual. With the great competition from mass-produced, inexpensive books, the individually produced picture book can remain in print only through continued library sales.

A librarian hands along to others what she has found significant, interesting, and beautiful in books. From the flood of picture books that pour off the presses each year it is increasingly difficult to select any that merit the designation "distinguished." In selecting and interpreting books for children,

A speech given at a meeting of the New York State Library Association in Syracuse, N.Y., 1949. Published in *The Horn Book,* September–October 1949.

librarians can actively encourage the production of good picture books. The problem of choosing good illustration in the books we give our children has many ramifications in our contemporary life.

A child can and must be trained in visual awareness if he is to become an aware adult. For the city child, there is the staccato excitement of geometry, subway lights, neon signs, sharp contrasts of light and shade, mass groupings of buildings and humanity. Human warmth becomes even more precious in such an atmosphere. For the country child, there are the subtle curves of landscape, a close-up of seasonal changes, the design of plant forms, a chance to observe the relationships of the parts of nature to the whole. Each child can be taught to enlarge his horizons.

Taste, the ability to discriminate, to cast off the false, the unworthy, and to retain the genuine; the capacity to see what is before us, to be alert; the pleasure in what is harmonious and at the same time various; the poise that is born of inner rhythm and balance—all these are best formed in early childhood. In our mechanized environment, mass media such as the comic book, the greeting card, magazine advertising, television, the motion picture, and the animated cartoon influence the visual perception of a child. The child's avidity for information, his need for excitement and adventure, his imagination, are exploited in this mass production of taste, with all its accompanying paraphernalia of saccharinity, sadism, and frenzied destruction. Now, added to this we have the mass-produced, inexpensive picture book that must cost as little as possible to produce and be easy to sell, since the motive for production is profit. Millions of copies of this type of book appear on the market each year. The public library, the school library, and the home—if in these places adults select good books for children—become islands in the flood. None of us would quarrel with the cost of these books to the children. Would that all their books could cost so little! But we can question their quality.

A picture book evolves from the combined effort of author, illustrator, publisher, and printer. All, I believe, are interested in producing a good book, but they must also produce a salable book. From our discussion we shall have to exclude the book produced entirely as a business commodity by huge combines and those concerns whose large reserves of funds afford them vast machines for production and distribution. The average publisher cannot afford to publish and keep in print a book that will not sell. And just as any united group of people accomplishes its work through a certain amount of personal compromise and mutual understanding of each other's needs and problems, so the production of a picture book entails concessions from one member of the group to another.

When the artist is also author, the chance for unity between text and pictures is usually greater, although it is conceivable that other artists could provide better illustrations than those of the author. Whether or not the author is artist, whether pictures and text form simultaneously in the author's mind or the writing of the text precedes the execution of the pictures, the problem of unity remains. For the pictures must be true to the spirit and feeling of the book as a whole, the spirit of the author's concept, and the child's acceptance. Once the artist has grapsed this concept, and this can happen in the short space of time needed to read the text because all his life has been a preparation for this moment, the plan of the book's appearance begins to take place in his mind. Perhaps he asks himself questions such as these:

What shape? How much space will I need for double spreads? Is the feeling of the book one of height, with tall buildings, trees that reach up, or is it horizontal, with long roads, the sea, a procession to stretch across a page? When Plato Chan had just finished the pictures for *Magic Monkey* he told us in the Children's Room of the New York Public Library that he made the book vertical because monkeys go up and down and *The Good-Luck Horse* horizontal because a horse is shaped that way.

What colors are appropriate to the story? Also, how many colors can the publisher afford to let me use? If I must use only two colors, what two will suggest the atmosphere of the story and provide one dark enough for a legible text? If the story has an exotic or a historical background, how much of the style determined by the background shall I use in my pictures? What technique shall I use: fine line, reed pen, watercolor, flat color, wash and line, crayon, spatter, linoleum cut, pastel and line? What typeface shall I keep in mind that will be harmonious with my drawings and also with the spirit of the book?

Each book presents a completely new set of problems. That is one reason why illustrating is such interesting work. Certain methods of reproduction are suitable to certain media, and the costs of these vary greatly. Just as the printmaker does not expect from an etching the same effect he can get in a wood block, so the illustrator cannot expect from line reproduction the nuances of a watercolor. An illustrator must acquaint himself with all these methods of reproduction to realize the best results from his work. His job does not end with the completion of his drawings, but only when the finished, bound book is in his hands. Many illustrators see their books through the entire ordeal of proving and printing.

To anyone who has taken the trouble to show fine paintings or reproductions to little children it should be apparent that there need be no condescension to their ages in the types of drawing and painting we offer them. They embrace all kinds and all subjects freely. Their own drawings may be realistic, near abstract, or conceptual. The child of six does not become lost in a tangle of associations and rules as he looks at a drawing. If its message is clear, whether simple or complex, he will comprehend it. Perhaps not all at once. But most worthwhile things bear more than one examination.

As for deciding which medium of illustration is best for children, the great variety of media and the many fine examples of each type prove the foolishness of dogmatism. The important question is what medium is best for this book, tells its message clearly—and is economically practicable. The photographs of *Tobe*, the colored wood blocks of Falls' *ABC*, the poster technique of LeWitt and Him in *Locomotive* and *The Little Red Engine Gets a Name*, Thomas Handforth's stylized pen line in *Tranquilina's Paradise* and his bold brush and crayon work in *Mei Li*, the black and white rhythmic line and mass of *Millions of Cats*, the beautiful abstract design of some of the Russian picture books of the '30's, the watercolors of *Little Tim and the Brave Sea Captain*, the colored lithographs of *A Child's Good Night Book*: these are just some of the media available to the illustrator. Why do many illustrators utilize so few of them?

Nor can we make rules about color in children's books, except that it be harmonious and appropriate to the subject. We have become so saturated with color in our advertising, in our magazine illustration, and in our motion pictures that we almost lose sight of the fact that children enjoy equally books with little or no color and books in full color. To refute the demand of those who want many colors, there are the richness of Wanda Gág's black-and-white drawings, the sepia of *Make Way for Ducklings*, the two colors of *Andy and the Lion*, *The Five Chinese Brothers*, and many others. Color is not so important as the richness of the message told by the illustrations in these books so well liked by children.

7

At a time when production costs are more than double what they were before the war, the illustrator is obliged to become more skilled in the utilization of small amounts of color. He must know how to get everything out of his colors through overlays in his color separations. Some illustrators, like Nicolas Mordvinoff, Roger Duvoisin, and Leo Politi, use two or three colors more effectively than others use five. The line drawings themselves must provide more color.

After the artist makes a dummy and has completed some of his final drawings, he may help select a typeface with the book designer or person in charge of manufacturing details. This type must be legible to children and harmonious with the pictures; it must fit into the proper space on the page and usually be available in linotype, since the cost of hand-set type is often prohibitive.

Before I worked on picture books I never realized the great number of manipulations that drawings and text go through before the completion of a book. I wish it were possible for everyone using books with children to observe a large offset press in operation, to see how negatives are made, how they are stripped up for making the final printing plates, and then to witness the actual printing of the large sheets that form the body of the book.

But from all the picture books produced, how are we to pick those that are exceptional? I believe that they must be regarded as are other forms of visual art. There is no recipe for judging illustration any more than there is a recipe for producing it.

It is extremely difficult to be objective about a picture book because each of us brings something different to what he sees. What is beautiful to one of us might be merely dull to another—or worse. Recently I gave a colored wood-block print to a friend in the hospital. The print was an abstraction of a mask in which I attempted to show two aspects of ennui, the giddy gaiety that tries to forget and the withdrawal into oneself. When the nurse's aide saw the print the next morning she said to my friend, "Miss, if you did that you deserve to be in the hospital! Them that can draw should draw pretty."

All that the artist has seen and felt deeply, his subconscious feelings and reactions to life, contribute to his work and will often be discernible there, setting up similar reactions in us as we look at it. Some illustrations set up reactions that continue long after we have ceased to look at them. Others we grasp at a glance because of the very narrow range of the experience they offer. Some books for children can be returned to again and again, not only because the child enjoys repetition, but because he will always find in them the reward of enjoyment.

Such books are those of the artist whose name is given to the greatest honor conferred on an illustrator of children's books, Randolph Caldecott. From the insipid, oversweet atmosphere of many of our picture books today, it is like stepping out of doors into a fresh wind to enter his picture books. Here are vitality in every line, sweep, humor without acerbity that never had to worry about age levels or suitability for children because it was born of rich observation of and enthusiasm for life itself. Here is such a thorough familiarity with the English countryside and its people that these scenes and characters could have sprung from no other soil. And all that is essential is clear to the youngest mind and yet stimulating to the adult who returns to it again and again. Much has happened in illustration and bookmaking since Caldecott's time, but the positive quality of his spirit remains in our best picture books.

In his *Last Lectures* Roger Fry suggests a method of examining works of art by confining attention to one or two qualities at a time and by comparing a number of different works to see to what extent they possess or lack these qualities. He chose sensibility and vitality. It might be profitable for us to study how these qualities can be reflected in the picture book.

The term sensibility includes two basic desires, the desire for order, harmony, and the desire for variety, chance, the unexpected. The first is expressed in the overall design of a work, the coordination of the parts in the whole. The other is subject to the feeling and sensitivity of the artist in executing the design or plan.

Since the picture book is a unit composed of text and pictures, I am assuming that the text of the book is at least good, if not distinguished in itself. Without making set rules only to break them, let us subject the visual elements that compose a picture book to an examination for those qualities Fry suggests. We can learn something from asking ourselves questions such as these:

How appropriate are the illustrations to the spirit as well as the facts of the story? If the illustrations are merely decorations, is this treatment all the story demands? Is there extraneous gingerbread in the decoration that might better have been left out? Do treatments vary from page to page, or are many pages monotonously alike in design? Do the margins allow enough air for the pictures to move in? If the page is bled, is it best that way?

Is the type legible and harmonious with the pictures and feeling of the story? Is there a pleasant visual play between pictures and type? Is the type attractively placed in relation to the pictures?

Is the color appropriate, interesting, or watered-down, sugary? If it is bright and harsh, is it appropriate so? We can expect bright color from a fire engine or a circus. How has the illustrator seen the whole book—in masses of color, in line, in rhythm? Why?

Is there a discernible buildup in the dramatic interest of the pictures as there is in the text? Is the characterization rich or meager, the people merely stereotypes, or do they have the qualities of individual human beings observable in life? Is there a buildup in characterization if the story requires it? Does the illustrator impose on us a reaction toward the characters that he wants us to feel? Does he nudge us to say, "This child, or this puppy, isn't he charming? Do you see what I mean?" If pushed too far we are apt to be aware of nothing but a sense of falseness.

How honest is the portrayal of various races and peoples? Do all of them resemble tinted Anglo-Saxons? What is the illustrator's feeling toward races other than his own? What appreciation of differences are we going to give our children? False generalizations about the goodness or evil of a race do little to create understanding.

Is the humor genuinely funny, or is it the tongue-in-cheek humor of the over-sophisticated adult?

How do the varieties of treatment reflect the sensibilities of the individual artist?

As we consider vitality we see how even more difficult it is to formulate any rules concerning this quality. Is there rhythm of line, of movement, of shape and mass in the drawings, and are these rhythms suitable to that of the story? If the text has sweep, do the pictures move likewise? Are the drawings so finished, so slick and photographically perfect that they were dead before we had a chance to look at them? This question is related to that of sensitivity of drawing. Do the drawings continue in the mind, as do those of Edy-Legrand, or are they so complete there is nothing for our minds and imaginations to do? Sheer virtuosity is often more useful in a juggler than in an artist. Is the drawing alive by itself on the page, as Andy and his lion are so thoroughly alive, or does it seem to live only because of its accurate resemblance to life? In his *The Spirit of Man in Asian Art* Laurence Binyon wrote, "The full mind, the rich mind, makes itself felt in the tracing of a few vivid lines; the empty mind, the poor nature, is betrayed in the most elaborate composition."

As we look at picture books we can find answers to all of these questions that will heighten our powers of discrimination. Perhaps the question that includes much of the foregoing could be—how rich is the experience in living the child gets, that I get, from looking at this book?

In their first books children begin to form their taste for art and literature. Anyone who has struggled to introduce mature writing to high school students saturated with comic books can appreciate this. It leads us into the question of our responsibility to children in training them to discriminate, to discard the cheap and ugly.

Perhaps exposure to good picture books in childhood will not assure an adult taste capable of appreciating fine art, but I do believe that a child unconsciously forms an approach to his visual world of order, rhythm, and interesting arrangements of color from the books he sees when young. The cleanness and simplicity of a well-designed page may start a chain of reactions that will continue into adulthood. If the child is accustomed to seeing varied and interesting shapes in his picture books, abstract art will not have the terrors for him that it seems to have for some adults. His discrimination, along with whatever of his individuality he can manage to preserve, will be his main defense against the bombardment of visual material on his eyes in most of his waking hours.

Librarians can play an important part in the future production of good books. They can select a few good picture books rather than many mediocre ones. We often forget that each year new groups of children are seeing for the first time books we have long known. Librarians can write to publishers about their reactions to books as they come out. They can award honors to books that are truly distinguished.

An author expects the librarian to bring some experience with literature to her judgment of a text. I feel that an illustrator or artist has a right to expect in those judging his work some art background. Just as an appreciation for great poetry is fed by great poetry and not by doggerel, so an appreciation of art must be fed by something more than book illustration. I know from experience how difficult it is to nourish an interest in painting if one lives in a small community, but through the state library, through art publications, it is possible at least to see reproductions of paintings of our own time, as well as earlier ones. Some of the paintings I remember best from my childhood are those reproduced on slides that my seventh-grade teacher obtained for us from the state library. Most of the names of the artists were forgotten until I met them again as an adult, but the images of the pictures remained.

If more adults were familiar with modern art movements and the problems artists today are trying to solve, we might hear fewer set conceptions and snap judgments of drawing and painting such as: "It's too modern! There's no perspective! I could draw as well myself and I can't draw a straight line! A child could do better!" Since art is a communication only in its own terms of line, color, and mass, we must learn to enjoy pictures with our senses instead of demanding logical explanations. It is senseless for us to be indifferent to art and to the training of children to see and select and then to deplore their lack of taste once they have become adults.

Let there be among librarians a wider examination of picture books of all types, past and present, American and foreign, so that their judgments will reflect a rich acquaintance with the whole field of illustration. Familiarity with some of the best picture books will show us how often we are content with the shoddy and the ordinary.

The effect of the popularity in America of Hollywood-inspired illustration is now coming back to us from Japan, France, Argentina, even from Switzerland—all countries that are also making beautiful books for children. Our responsibility to children does not stop with our own boundaries. We must show to other countries the best we have to offer.

In judging I believe we should leave our personal prejudices for the illustrator or subject out of consideration. If an award is to be given to a distinguished book, let it be given to just that, the book that will carry the seal of your recognition to the public. If a picture book does not wear well, can't we rightly ask ourselves, was it ever really good, or merely timely? The book itself has not changed.

This awarding of honors has an effect on other librarians who do not have an opportunity to see much of a year's output of books, as they buy for school and public libraries, as they suggest purchases to parents. It has a great effect on bookstore sales and the production of similar books by publishers. A great part of the public is impressed by prizes and slavishly follows the edicts of the critics and book reviewers, instead of judging for itself. Most people have neither time nor opportunity to examine large numbers of children's books, even if they were interested. They rely on the judgment of those they consider experts.

Awards have an effect on the artists themselves. It has always been the fate of some artists to be either misjudged or to feel that their best work is unrecognized. Often an artist receives recognition for work inferior to what he has done previously.

Librarians can demand high standards from their illustrators and publishers. Why is it that as we examine the output of many of our outstanding illustrators we find so few who have grown appreciably since their first books? A story about a child of 1800, one of 1949, one in Mexico, one in Alaska—all get the same illustrative treatment from them. Their growth has been in perfecting what they already could do rather than in experimenting and reaching out into new fields. Perhaps we have directly or indirectly asked these artists to repeat themselves. An illustrator must produce what sells in order to live. But to do his best work he must also be free to listen to his own inner voice and act upon it. Many illustrators are doing other artwork as well as illustration in order to work in complete freedom. By buying only work that resembles an illustrator's earlier books we force him to stunt himself to our prescription. Let us encourage him to grow, to experiment, to try new techniques, by being at least receptive to the new.

INTEGRITY
AND INTUITION

*"A picture book really exists only when
a child and a book come together. . . ."*

An artist cannot help feeling deeply honored to receive an award bearing the name of Randolph Caldecott, one of the happiest spirits in children's books. Prizes and awards seem to be gifts from the gods, unless they are given for measurable performances, such as jumping. Perhaps this one has been given for sheer persistence in running up. The book so honored is neither better nor worse than it was before, but the illustrator has grown in that you have added to her your confidence in her and her work.

It is also a great pleasure to receive an award given by librarians. Public libraries have been a part of my life as long as I can remember. When our family moved to a new town, my sisters and I made a trip to the library to make friends with the librarian and get our library card before our parents had a chance to unpack the china. One of the first books that came

Caldecott Medal acceptance speech for *Cinderella*, given at the annual conference of the American Library Association in Philadelphia, Pa., on July 5, 1955. Published in *The Horn Book*, August 1955.

home from the library in Cooperstown was *Clean Peter and the Children of Grubbylea,* suggested purposely, I am afraid, by an older sister. We were near enough of an age to share a pleasure in the same books. One night when I was five and she and I were alone, to amuse me she read aloud Andersen's fairy tales. Three of us sat in our old, black leather Morris chair—she on one side, our good-sized Airedale on the other, and I in the middle, feeling the warmth of each as an antidote to the sadness of "The Little Match Girl."

I shall never forget our excitement when later on we discovered *Otto of the Silver Hand.* Any child brought up on Howard Pyle and the Lang fairy books can hardly help acquiring some feeling for the Middle Ages. Reading books and listening to music were as normal parts of my childhood as eating and playing. I can never look on those Carnegie buildings in small towns—the red brick, the golden oak, the cool, dim corners behind potted palms, the smell of the stamping pads, the peculiar, cozy smell of worn buckram and pages that felt as soft as old flannel—without thinking of what that place is meaning to some child who thinks of it as a second home, a kind of last stand of privacy.

On the top floor of that library in Cooperstown was a small museum, containing, among others, two wonderful things— one, an exact model of James Fenimore Cooper's house. "Through the little windows you could look right into the rooms." The whole thing seemed a glorified dollhouse to my sisters and me, who spent a good deal of time leaning on the table, looking in those windows and imagining a life inside. I always had a passion, like Tag-a-long Too-Loo's, for little things, chiefly boxes and dolls. The other wonderful object in that museum was a primitive little doll carved by an Eskimo from walrus ivory. She was only about two and a half inches high and had almost no face. I wondered if she was aware of my devotion or of the many trips I made to the library just to go upstairs alone to look at her. Like most children, I never told my love.

No one can know the influence on a child of those first books and their pictures, good and bad. Reproductions were then all I saw of the great paintings of the world. Most of these were on slides borrowed from the state library by a wise and enterprising seventh-grade teacher who, when we were restless, would often suddenly say, "I think we need some slides." Down would come the dark curtains of the schoolroom windows, and off that seventh grade went, transported and refreshed by *The Wedding of Aurora* or Botticelli's *Primavera*.

From the time when I first wanted to illustrate books, and that was quite early in my life (it all seemed more possible somehow when we moved to the parsonage where Maud Petersham had lived as a girl), I was interested in books for younger rather than older children. The greater attractiveness of those I saw in the former group and the often disappointing dullness of those I saw in the latter made me feel that way. I remember a keen resentment that a book was illustrated at all when the pictures were inadequate compared to those pictures that formed in the mind.

A young child shares with the primitive an extraordinary power to identify himself with the people, animals, and things of this world, and this power makes him extremely accessible to the magic power of symbol. This same power carried into adult life enables the artist to enter the feelings of his subjects and draw and paint them in such a way that not only do they look as if they felt a certain way, but they also make the spectator feel that same way. Young children have a profound sense of the mysterious, but if the mood of our work is to speak to them, it must relate to other realities they know. The child cannot gape forever at the juggler or shiver endlessly

21

with the tightrope walker. After the circus is over the arc of his own ball in the air will be more beautiful, the sureness of his own foot as he walks the curb will give him pride. He contains his experience.

A picture book really exists only when a child and a book come together, when the stream that formed in the artist's mind and heart flows through the book and into the mind and heart of the child. Before starting to make the book, an artist must be sure the story is worth the time, his time and love spent in illustrating it, and the child's time to be spent in looking at it.

Once the story is chosen, what is its texture? What are the large patterns of action? These might be the very meaning of the story itself.

A picture book is somewhat related in its effect to that of a painting. The whole is greater than any of its parts, but all the parts must relate directly to each other in harmony. The young child might be more receptive to the intuition of the artist than the educated adult, who might be an ignoramus in art, for all his conscious knowledge. But the pictures must be blessed with real intuitive quality for them to speak to him.

The clearest exposition of the creative process I have yet found is Jacques Maritain's *Creative Intuition in Art and Poetry*, in which he tells of inspiration (and those who scoff at its necessity to a work perhaps have never felt it) springing from the dark night of the soul in vibrations that he calls "pulsations," "wordless songs," then assuming form as one begins to think of the work in question, and finally being subjected to conscious reason. As an artist develops he gradually becomes aware of the presence of this night, and learns to trust in it; for it is there, not at the surface of his mind, which deals with the problems of existence, but deep in those waters that contain the resources of his spirit and intellect, that his intuition has its birth. That is why, I think, when only vague feelings are beginning to form, an artist should be left alone to let them gradually rise to the surface and take form as visual ideas. And that is also why the feeling of others can hardly be incorporated or even listened to at this point if the finished work is to have the integrity which means that it sprang from an artist's own sensibility. His sensibility, of course, has been enriched by his thinking, his seeing, his feeling, his living—all his life up to now, and that is what is drawn on, not the impulses of last week. That might be another reason why the time spent on creating a book in its first form, that is, making the dummy if there is to be a visual plan, can be very short or very long. I have never been impressed by tales of the extraordinary length of time that it took to produce books or paintings. An art student's laborious drawing of a month will not compare with a one-minute impression of a Picasso. All one's life has been spent in preparation for the work at hand. When the greatest amount of inspiration is brought to bear, the least amount of work will bring the idea to realization. Inspiration—no minute in making a work should escape it.

In our modern world beauty is often dismissed in favor of hard labor. People will respect the hours consumed in a project without ever questioning the use of the time spent in the first place.

The artist is overcharged and works to find a relief, ease for his burden, so that he can take up another as soon as he is able. At his most relaxed he is often most unhappy; at his most tense, difficult as he might be to live with, he is often experiencing one of his deepest joys, for he is finding his way back into himself. This region is so subjective that he is often hardly aware it existed, but he knows, if he has listened to music, that it exists in others. Rhythms he feels there are old as time and tide, but they are part of the bloodstream of all the morning subway riders. Colors take their meaning from first awareness of light, blue vastness of sea and sky, hot warmth of fire, the sun, and his own blood. Sounds, movements, all these rise to the surface to be called into use to speak to the same feelings in another human being. These feelings or this intuition, if it is strong enough in a person, demands to be expressed in work, even if that work is never understood by others. Its strength is such that it will drive an artist to live the life of greatest hardship in order to nourish it and allow it to have its way with him.

The question of integrity has a direct bearing on one's choice of subject matter for a book. Who knows when an idea can light a match? A sight of children playing in a city street; meeting a stalwart Cape-Codder of three who that day had fallen off a dock when the tide was in and had walked in to shore, as his brother told us, "by hisself"; hearing an old rhyme read or a sly old folk tale; or having one's editor suggest illustrating a tale, the feeling of which, if not the exact images, had persisted in the mind since early childhood; any reason can exist, it seems, for making a picture book. But, and this I believe most strongly, the reasons have to be a part of the person and his feeling before he attempts the book. Contrivance and fad-following impress only those who are unaware of their superficiality.

A good editor knows the stage at which authors and artists must be left alone if their work is to be their own best expression. I have been most fortunate in my editor, Alice Dalgliesh. As an outstanding writer for children, and a very kind friend, she has given me more than usual understanding and consideration during times of stress.

The whole process of actually getting a picture book ready for the printer usually takes me about five months. It is sometimes difficult to maintain the same high pitch of excitement that was there when the work started, but it must be done. The original idea must always be the aim. In almost all cases, it is the one with vitality and truest feeling toward the text.

Why is it that the paintings of children often have qualities of intensity of expression, beauty of color, and depth of feeling that make us feel that they are works of art? By his desire to say something, to force the meager means, the meager knowledge at his disposal, the child is able to draw what he has to say so vividly that his drawing speaks to us. All during the work on a book, all during his working life, the artist will be forcing *his* means to say what he has to say. The means will always be determined by the subject at hand, and that is why I feel that each book should look different from the others, whether or not the medium used is the same.

The simplicity of a very young child's pleasure in a little street carousel, a tale of a roguish cat that is colored by the sophistication of the Sun King's Court, the longing and immolation of a little tin soldier, the freshness of a lovely young girls's dream as opposed to her stepsisters' delusions of grandeur, and they more waspish than wicked—how could one feel the same about such different books? A technique learned as a formula to apply willy-nilly to any subject often knocks the life out of the subject. The vitality, the quality peculiar to the subject should dictate the method to follow. Is the subject to yield to the manner, or the manner to the subject?

Whatever the means, the only pictures that will arouse interest and love in a child are those created in the same interest and love. Each word, each gesture counts toward giving the fullest value of the feeling. White space, in which the mind rests or fills in its own images, can be as telling as drawing and will certainly be more effective than empty decoration. Research is done simply to aid in picturing the idea, bringing it into objective being, never for its own sake. Incompletely absorbed research results in costume plates or journalism, not creation. How do the colors speak in this telling, not how many colors are there? One accent rightly placed, whether color, shape, or line, can be worth a hundred small forms. One small area can suggest the design of a whole curtain. The mind continues where the pictures end.

A horse is not drawn in a stroke or two because the artist wanted to show his skill. But, feeling strongly, he got the horse down fast, and there it was—in two or three lines. Why add more and get the horse ready for the taxidermist?

We often hear it said of an artist that he or she has developed no personal style yet. One of the most unfortunate pressures put on young artists in this country that sets such a premium on novelty, often while the artist is still in art school, is to develop a distinguishing style to apply to his work.

To me style is the way you walk and talk, what you are as a person. The discerning eye will notice certain traits of personality, certain ways of feeling that will show up in the work. These help to make a person's style, not a technique that is put on like a garment. *Style,* in the larger sense, is something quite different. We live in a world eager for recipe or formula, which, not finding it, hands over its birthright of independent thinking to the self-styled expert who imagines he has it. Any effort to coddle originality is to end by stifling it in self-consciousness. An artist's primary preoccupation is his own *development,* the perfection of himself as an instrument—whether he be singer, dancer, or painter—the better to sing his song. He is faced with all of life, but the mirror he holds up to it can be no bigger than his own mind and heart.

I have never felt that children needed any particular kind of drawing any more than they needed any particular kind of writing. The clarity, vitality of the message, the genuineness of the feeling—that is what is important.

After a book is done, it passes from the artist and has a completely separate and, we hope, strenuously active life of its own in the hands of children. But now it is something apart. Only by putting the feelings that were specifically tied up with it completely out of mind will the artist be free to be ready for something else, to grow by feeling all over again, by trying to look at the new book as if he had never done another. To forget the old solutions, to refuse to copy not only what he has seen but also his own work is one of the greatest problems of an artist, but only by meeting its challenge can he avoid his own clichés.

I have always felt that good drawing is more important than color in a young child's book. Yet color and its symbolism speak very directly to children. Color is often most rich when it means something perhaps too subjective to be put into words, when it is the expression of some life value. Only a hypothetical child brought up in a hypothetical vacuum without the sense of sight, even without that marvelous sight behind the eyelids that little chidren know in their daydreams, could be impervious to the meanings of color. These meanings are old as life itself. The passion of little children for red has an earthy origin not to be denied. Blue sky, blue sea, green-and-brown earth, red fire—their world radiates from very simple color relationships. By color they can be led into a greater sensual enjoyment of the visible world, as well as that between the covers of their books.

The choice of a color combination for a picture book will often have been associated with the book from its first imaginings.

Gold of the summer fields, gold of a small boy's thatch of hair, gold of his dream of London, the sunrise when he heard

27

his destiny ring out in Bow Bells, gold of his treasure and of the chain of his office of Lord Mayor—gold was the color for Dick Whittington.

When I was in the Virgin Islands, the unbelievable turquoise water of the Caribbean, the mahogany-skinned people, brilliant white sand, coral-colored houses and bougainvillea, deep green of welcome shadow, chartreuse of leaves filtering sunlight—the colors for *Henry-Fisherman* chose themselves.

The colors for *The Steadfast Tin Soldier* I felt could speak to children on several levels. "Red and blue was their beautiful uniform." " . . . a bright spangle as big as the whole of her face." Red, blue, and gold, and black for type became a blue-violet that could tell of steadfastness, infinite longing; the red became rose for passion and sacrifice; the gold a minute glitter on the surface; black became charcoal for the somber note of the troll's warning and the ash in which were found the little tin heart and the burnt black spangle.

But how to get all one's colors to speak? In the past few years we have seen more and more books using a crayon-and-line technique, with the drawings reproduced directly from the artist's own color separations by means of a contact method with no camera work. Any process that throws the illustrator back on his own resources is good for him, because if he is not to do the same book over and over, regardless of the subject, he must push what he knows farther and farther in order to encompass the feeling of the new work at hand. By making their own plates, by exploring the variety of effects possible with hand-graphic techniques, illustrators can develop the freedom of fine artists in their printmaking. Color separations are a step, a crucial one, in a long creative process that begins with feeling and should end with feeling. Illustrators are engaged in making books that are usually collections of offset lithographs, not originals that a printer must print exactly. In America we have just begun to tap the vast resources of the medium. The highly imaginative approach of artists like Roger Duvoisin, Nicolas, and Hans Fischer is an inspiration to the rest of us. In his color separations the artist has a chance to correct, to simplify, always with the aim to get back and clarify his first dreams, never to "finish." When a work is completely finished it is dead. What can the child or anyone else bring to it that will complete the feeling and give it second life? By work the artist effaces traces of work. It is not pleasant for us to agonize with him. We care nothing for the hours he took. Why does he bother us with them? Let's hear his story now, listen to his song.

My editor, Alice Dalgliesh, and the distinguished art director at Scribners, Margaret Evans, have been as anxious as I to make picture books as beautiful as ingenuity and budget will allow. A beautiful type page, quality of binding cloth, color harmonizing with, playing against, or repeating a color in the book, a cover stamp that conveys some of the spirit of the book, endpapers, if used, that both summarize and introduce the mood of the story or in design and color set a period—all these details help to make a book what it is. In spite of ever-increasing bindery and production costs, artist, editor, and designer look on their work as a challenge. The end in view is always to make the book a unified and beautiful object, each part expressive of the spirit of the whole, each part complementing the other toward this end.

The book as a beautiful object will pass from our scene unless children and adults are taught to love and appreciate it. Today, institutions and products that were brought into being because of some individual's intense personal interest are being leveled out to meet the demands of a hypothetical universal public taste, under the mistaken notion that you can please all the people all of the time. It is very discouraging to an artist to hear that schools and libraries often buy unbound sheets, have them "prebound" in covers of color and texture not only out of harmony with the feeling of the book but often downright ugly. How can a child sense the loving care that went into the creation of this book? The argument given for such a practice is that the book will last longer. But figures tell us that thus bound it costs almost twice as much. Why not give the child the book as it was originally planned and when it wears out give him another fresh copy?

When I was a child, thinking that I would like one day to illustrate books for children, I always thought of the fairy tales that I loved. It was some years before I felt ready or capable of attempting illustrations for Andersen or Perrault. When an illustrator attempts the interpretation of a folk or fairy tale that already stands as an entity, the problem of adding a new dimension and bringing the whole into harmonious unity is great. Illustration becomes a kind of visual storytelling in the deepest sense of the word. As a storyteller ideally submerges himself in the story until he loses his own identity and becomes a medium for the revelation of the story, the illustrator must likewise submerge himself in the feeling, so that what comes through is an interpretation and intensification of meanings. The big meanings, the big masses, big movements and rhythms must hold the same relationships as in oral telling. Rhythm of speech is echoed in rhythm of line and color. Never must there be a mere recounting of the event. None of these things may be consciously aimed at; yet I feel they are part of the illustrator's feeling as he attempts to make a picture storybook of a fairy tale. The pictures can convey the wonder, terror, peace, mystery, beauty—all he is able to feel or might convey if he were telling the story in words.

The popularity of certain types of subject matter rises and falls, but children remain basically the same, with the same gaiety, eagerness to feel, the same clear-eyed wisdom and wonder in facing the world. Educators and experts on child study, who sometimes seem to have been as supple as straws in the wind, quick to bend to this or that breeze or fad, for a time decided that children no longer needed fairy tales. Not for a moment did the children who came of their own accord to public libraries and were free to choose their own books, desert their heroes, the personification of their dreams. The calls still came for *Cinderella,* for stories about giants and princesses, for simple people raised to high station because of their own gifts. Some of these stories appeared horrifying to adults, who seemed to lack the balance of the children in these matters. The children looked beyond the horror to the battle between moral forces. The heritage of childhood is the sense of life bequeathed to it by the folk wisdom of the ages. To tell in pictures, to tell in words, to tell in dance—however we may choose—it is a privilege to pass these truths on to children who have a right to the fullest expression we can give them. Neither so self-conscious as a parable nor so contrived as an allegory, fairy tales are revelations of sober everyday fact. They are the abiding dreams and realities of the human soul.

This very day some rogue has by his quick wit opened a new world to his master and helped him win the princess of his heart, to whom he was entitled by sensibilities if not by birth.

Today a staunch soldier, through circumstances not of his own making, goes through terrible trials but remains steadfast in his devotion to his ideal.

Tonight somewhere Cinderella, through the magic of kindness, has been enchanted into greatest beauty; tonight Cinderella goes to her ball to meet her prince.

BIG AND LITTLE

*"Can we ever stop thinking about big—
to think once more about little?"*

Seven years ago I was in the same predicament of trying to express adequately to you my appreciation of your recognition of my work. Seven was always magical; but when the seven comes between one and two, the magic has been more than doubled.

In 1932 Luigi Pirandello wrote to his friend Bontempelli: "Can I say something to you in confidence? I know that you are a judge in the Premio Viareggio. I read the list of contestants . . . and already the problem of the young winner gives me anguish. To be born is easy; to be born in art was always less so. The great venture of every artist is, on the contrary then, when he is born, to live—to continue to live."

Seven years can bring a person to a time in which the initial impetus that started him in his career has altered in direction or intensity, when his understanding and experience are greater, but his energy is undeniably less, and all the clocks run faster. When I was working on *Once a Mouse . . .* , I sus-

Caldecott Medal acceptance speech for *Once a Mouse . . .*, given at the annual conference of the American Library Association in Miami Beach, Fla., on June 19, 1962. Published in *The Horn Book,* August 1962.

35

pected that it might be my best book to date. To have you recognize it is more than doubly precious to me.

I had wanted a big subject, with few words, that would say something to a little child, and in which I could immerse myself fully. Since I had been making colored wood blocks, I wanted a theme to which colored woodcuts would add another dimension. All fall of 1960 I had been drawing at the Bronx Zoo, magnetized particularly by the tigers in the Lion House and the monkeys. Then a friend sent me a collection of animal fables, published in Italy. Here I found the ancient Indian fable of "The Hermit and the Mouse," and my big subject for little children. The very fiber of wood might say something about a hermit and animals in a jungle.

I have always felt that a good book comes from an individual sensibility, or from one of those blessed unions when two act as one. But a finished book can hardly be the work of one person, especially the trade book with a rigid production budget for whatsoever book of the same size. For reasons known only to their creators, some books are not at all "whatsoever" to the person who is making them; and he is fortunate indeed if his editors recognize this, too.

When I showed my usual little dummy to Morrell Gipson, I received that most precious of go-aheads from any editor, complete liberty to develop the book as I felt it. Margaret Evans, art editor of Scribners, believed in the book. How can one be grateful enough to work with one who, having control over the ultimate look of a book, demonstrates a will to integrity in everything she touches, which generally means everything to do with the physical book? You who make books know how challenging and often dismaying it is to work within the limits of the trade book today. Almost every desire to communicate on a plane other than that of words and pictures is thwarted. I am very grateful to my publishers, Charles Scribner's Sons, for many things, but especially for their trying their utmost to maintain a high standard in book production. Design still includes the whole book and not just the inside pages. Some librarians have expected all things of all books, confusing books for leisure reading with textbooks, have made almost impossible demands for stronger bindings, out of all proportion to the normal use of a book and to the strength of the paper on which it is printed. Costs, naturally, have risen, and librarians have met the publisher's complaints of distress with protests at the cost of his books. Unless these demands are tempered, and sights are set, not on technical details such as durability of bindings, but on the life of a book in the mind and heart of a child and not only in his hands, the book as we have been privileged to make it, to use it, to share it, will cease to exist. It is disappearing fast. Like the Pobbles, we shall probably have no toes, and possibly taste will be so degraded that few will know the difference. But the effect will have been felt by the children.

The "will to integrity" was a Gibraltar. Margaret Evans has a craftman's patience with things but is an artist, with an artist's quick comprehension of another's intent. For some time we had wondered what could be done if an illustrator might work on his own plates at the printers. Reehl Lithographers could not have given us more friendly cooperation. In order to preserve the texture as well as the outline of the blocks, the book was finally printed from contact plates made from my prints on very thin tissue.

Painters today have unlimited freedom in the choice of techniques and an almost fetishistic interest in sensuous materials. But no matter how fascinated an illustrator is by techniques, illustrating must still be that—a servant charged with elucidating the idea of the book. It involves a very different mental process from painting and arises from a different level of sensibility. A little child's own art is emblematic but often falls short of the ideal in his mind. Recognition of species only—man with two legs, dog with four—is not enough to stimulate his awakening sense of personality. The child will have to make his home in the astonishing world of the future that is beginning to erupt about us. How complete is the personality that he takes from us into that future? His books help to make it.

Can you listen once more to a very free retelling of the fable of the hermit and the mouse?

You could call it *Once a Hermit.* . .

A long time ago, before the days of "togetherness" in the literary jungle, most publishers were hermits—meditative, often mighty at magic, and, once in a while, mighty at prayer. Some wore beards, all wore at least a loincloth, and green was the color of the leaves of the trees. The hermit publisher lived in comparative peace in the jungle, amid the lions, the dogs, the jackals, and the nightingales.

But in a corner of the publishing hut there was a little mouse that the hermit had rescued—rescued from "peeps" and "glimpses" and "little excursions" into little-known places. The hermit nourished him with fresh experiences and fed him with fantasy, and the little mouse grew.

But look! One night, down the highroad and over the bridge to the crossroads, hovered the shadow of three owls, with their sights set high and their great eyes focused—straight on the hermit-publisher's mouse.

When he looked up and saw the danger threatening his little pet, the hermit said, among other things, a little prayer, and toughened his mouse. It became a stout cat (with a future in millions and billions and trillions of kittens).

Days and nights came and went. The cat grew handsome

(on good paper and good typography), grew playful, grew wise, possessed a normal vocabulary of purrs but also knew how to use its claws. Children who came to play often went away wiser.

By now the forest was full of owls. Many, fortunately, were still flying high, but some had set their sights lower and were becoming more expert all the time. They blinked more during the day, saw some things double and many things not at all— or at least much less clearly than their three ancestors. Some became shortsighted and were apt to swoop on the first thing they saw. The cat had a horrid feeling that they were after his skin! They were a real challenge to the cat and his master.

Then one night a cash register was heard to jingle in the jungle. The cat ran under the bed, but the publisher opened one eye. Then they both listened, and they liked the sound. And the hermit, who hadn't quite arrived at thinking about big, thought less about little. "Expand!" he cried, and the cat became a big dog. Now, when the dog barked, it was the cash register that listened.

Then an explosion shook the world, and the jungle felt the reverberations. Hungry hucksters prowled in the jungle, seduced some of the painters and nightingales, bedazzled or silenced forever some of the owls, and then leaped on the dog.

The hermit was already unnerved by the hootings of fearful owls. He lost his head. He forgot who he was and why he was. He also forgot what was his dog. With a gesture to improving him, he changed the dog into a handsome tiger.

Superficially, the tiger resembled the cat, but he was much more blown up. His coat was brilliant, decorated by the most publicized artists. But he was hamstrung; his legs moved in only one direction—ahead. He roared in yelps to beginners beginning to be beginning. He frightened no one, though, for the hermit, remembering that the cat's claws had made careful children cautious, had filed the claws of the tiger down to the pads. And every time he stepped off the path, the owls descended on him like hawks.

But you don't have to imagine the pride of the tiger. It was quite apparent. He fed on firsts and mosts and bests. He littered in so many new series a year that he couldn't always give much thought to the last of his litters. He lorded it over the other animals, because those taller than he had all been cut down.

People who came to look marveled at his size. "And to think that that tiger was once a mouse!" they said. The tiger was humiliated at this. He decided to destroy the hermit. But the hermit saw red. Quickly consolidating his forces and funds, he ceased altogether to be a hermit, leaped on the tiger's back, and rode him off into the jungle.

As for the children, they, too, had been hypnotized by all that brightness, charmed by those roars. Around a pool in the forest, many sat all day, gazing at their own reflections. They called into caverns, listening for the sound of their own voices. Many couldn't get over their beginning. They passed with averted faces the pens where the hobbled heroes were kept—the cages of the eagles with clipped wings, the soiled swans—to enter their private tunnels through the undergrowth. Because they had so little time for wandering, they liked their tunnels straight. And the tunnels often emptied into deserts, from which they could set their sights on distant stars, having lost interest in their own.

And now, at the end of the spring, there is a great gathering of birds in the palms by the sea at the edge of the jungle: hawks and magpies, warblers and crows, larks and doves. They plan, they sing, they celebrate. But the owls that have not turned ostrich, the owls that think ahead to the fall and winter, that have seen the retreat of the hermit, ask each other, "Is it partly our fault that he rides his tiger deeper and deeper into the jungle? Can he remember anymore how it was to be a hermit? Can he ever stop thinking about big—to think once more about little?"

THE HERO WITHIN

*". . . What was feared, that final gift of one's spirit,
the total risk of oneself, is a key that will
unlock life to them, will reveal the hero within."*

W hen I was asked to speak to you today, the invitation
brought back to me the days when, just out of college, I went
to a small town in New York State to teach English to high-
school students and became a member of the National Council of Teachers of English. I knew nothing, really, about the
organization but felt at least some kind of bond, if only in a
shared love of literature, with other teachers of English.

I suspect all of us here started out in some way fired by the
books we had read, ignited perhaps by some imaginative
teacher who swept us up in his own enthusiasm. I wonder if
a real love for books was ever transmitted from teacher to
child without the catalyst of enthusiasm.

And now, today, I am meeting with you, having come here
very much by a backdoor route, for most of my adult life no
longer a teacher, but sharing with you a feeling for children
and books.

Speech given at the annual conference of the National Council of Teachers
of English in Houston, Tex., November 1966. Published in *Elementary English,*
March 1967.

This tale that I am about to tell you is of a little boy who lived and suffered in the dark middle ages; of how he saw both the good and the bad of men, and of how, by gentleness and love and by strife and hatred, he came at last to stand above other men and to be looked up to by all. . . .

Otto's life was a stony and a thorny pathway, and it is well for all of us nowadays that we walk it in fancy and not in truth.

So back in 1888 Howard Pyle wrote his introduction to *Otto of the Silver Hand*. Forty years later I read *Otto* and thrilled to the most satisfying of illustrations for me then. For Pyle pictured a solid world, with evil faced and drawn, and purity of spirit glinting out from those illustrations.

Almost forty years later—the other day—I reread the book. I was not surprised that it was for many years a favorite.

It is hard to say just what effect the books we read in childhood have on our later life, but we all know they do have an effect—in images that will not be erased, in people as real as those we know, in conversations heard as echoes, as the conversation in the abbey belfrey between young Otto and the simple Brother John, who had seen the angel Gabriel:

"But tell me, Brother John," said little Otto, in a hushed voice, "what else did the good angel say to thee?"

Brother John stopped short in his song and began looking from right to left, and up and down, as though to gather his wits.

"So!" said he, "there was something else that he told me. Tschk! If I could but think now. Yes, good! This is it—'Nothing that has lived,' said he, 'shall ever die, and nothing that has died shall ever live.' "

From those days the emphasis has changed in many of our children's books. A child then often seemed small and weak in a world of brutal adult hatreds. Otto was caught in the baronial wars of medieval Germany. But the story of his growth in character is as much his father's as it is his.

The little child walks about his small world in a long shadow. He clasps his hands behind his back, he struts, a mimic of his father. He tends his doll, furnishes his playhouse, and plays his mother. His theatre is diminutive, a chamber opera of strong feelings played out on a small stage.

He roars like a lion—or a truck—drives like a plane, curls up like a cat. There is no limit to his impersonations. His older brother, who may be in the fourth grade, is already a man to him. He ambushes foes, flies missions over dangerous territory, rockets to the moon, and, as often as not, comes when he is called in to supper. Policeman, garbage man, Batman— the characters who walk into that chamber from the street or the screen give him a yardstick for his own measure.

He grows—and looks—and listens—and chooses—and blends with the crowd that presses onto his ever-widening stage. He grows—and the characters he counts closest are fewer, are apt to be his own age. The older ones recede into the background; their words and calls echo across ever widening spaces: "Come back!" "Have a good time!" "Be careful!" "Why did you do it?"

The stage shrinks—the lights pick out only a few characters; and eventually in the dark is left one—having a dialogue with one—facing the mirror that strips off the outer skin and leaves the self.

And there the real tournament begins, there the slaying of the monster, there the scaling of the precipice. The flare of the cloak, the flash of armor, the blare of trumpets are left far behind. The once-child arises, staggered from this dialogue, to step into the drama of his adult life.

The arena of his mature struggle will be one of feeling and spirit, as well as thought, and the choices he will make will sound the keynote of that dialogue as he seeks his fathers, his heroes, his gods within himself.

We are in a period of explosions, of change, of thrusts into the future that leave much of our past in contempt. Contempt for the ancestor, for the elder, for the parent passes very quickly into contempt for all our past. We see it in our commercial exploitation and adoration of the young, in our art forms that appear to make earlier forms meaningless, in our disregard of our history.

We have brought young people up in an idealism that they often find ill-fitted to the world that is. D. H. Lawrence, in his *Studies in Classic American Literature,* uses a most striking image—of American ideals rusted like armor into the flesh, impossible either to put off or to use as curb to willful action.

The frenzy of some young people to throw over controls of any sort might come from a profound disillusionment with the controls placed on them—too strong, too weak, too impossible to be reasonable. The dreams that satisfied their elders we know full well may not be theirs. On the one side they howl defiance to drown out what they hear as lies; on the other, they are scared to death. Those who have never found their hero within—and we sometimes see their pictures in the newspapers, with their eyes canceled out in black, affirming their anonymity in legion—needed heroes long before those pictures had to be taken. Each time we offer a child gadgetry and tricks in his books instead of spirit, we show our mistrust of him and deprive him of his chance for self-identification. I suspect that many children dislike what they call "I" books because such books force them to remain outside the characters. "I" is a person who is not the reader.

In the fullness of its energy and courage, youth hardly knows a limit to its strength. Heroism is often as natural to its surging vitality as the plunge to save a swimmer overcome in the surf. But once that vitality ebbs, the hero's tread is not so often the clank of the mailed foot on the castle floor as the almost noiseless one-foot-before-the-other of every day.

To quote Gerard Manley Hopkins:

O the mind, mind has mountains, cliffs of fall
Frightful, sheer, no-man-fathomed. Hold them cheap
May who ne'er hung there. . . .

To be true to the hero one has felt growing within one from the beginning—when the horizon is marked, when one has faced the limits of one's ability, one's strength, one's capacity to act, the conventional comforts of religious systems—there begins the real test of heroism. Heroism—a billow, a flare of spirit rather than of banners, an armor of patience forged of the steel of backbone and will to make one's living, a life.

Of all the forces that shape a child, that rub off his edges and round his corners until he fits smoothly into the holes prescribed by our society, perhaps books are more important than we know. They act on a creature enacting as well as living his life, as he starts out on the long struggle to make of himself a human being.

Mesmerized by the charm of the little child, we sometimes fill his room with mirrors instead of windows. We sometimes forget that he is seed and bud and that the full flowering of his maturity is our main concern. The fruit must be allowed to ripen, slowly, naturally. We hear a good deal about the word *creativity,* often from people who least understand its mysteries. Childhood must take in more than it gives out.

A great writer and one of the most perceptive of human beings, Colette, wrote this in her journal:

My childhood and my free and solitary adolescence were equally preserved from the urge to express myself, both periods being uniquely occupied in directing their subtle antennae toward what can be contemplated, heard, touched, breathed. O deserts, fenced in and without dangers, footprints of bird and hare on snow, ponds covered with ice or veiled with the warm mists of summer, assuredly you gave me as many joys as I could hold. Should I call my school a school? Rather, it was a kind of rude paradise where disheveled angels chopped wood in the morning to light the stove, and ate, instead of celestial manna, thick slices of plain farm bread on which they spread a paste of kidney beans that had been cooked in red wine. There was no railway in my part of the country, no electricity, no college or big city nearby. In my family, there was no money, but there were books; no gifts, but there was tenderness; no comfort, but we had freedom. No voice borrowed the sound of the wind to whisper in my ear, along with a gust of cold air, the advice to write and write, to dim by writing about it my thrilling or tranquil perception of the living universe.

Like the young hero who saw strange and wonderful things on Mulberry Street, like Max, setting off in his wolf suit to *Where the Wild Things Are,* a child generally makes a distinction in his mind between fantasy and reality. He will indulge his ego with earthbound fantasies in the so-called realistic books. But fairy-tales, myths, and legends will lead him ever beyond the ego's reach and extend his perception of the actual.

I saw the familiar coonskin cap and a wigwam in front of the baroque church on a Venetian canal, as a grandmother watched her charges act out their desperate games. In the Luxembourg gardens, there was the same coonskin cap, a shield of valor for the pale and shy child who wore it, powerful as Perseus' hat of darkness in the Greek myth.

So Jason and the Argonauts, facing the six-armed giants:

Each of these monsters was able to carry on a whole war by himself, for with one of his arms he could fling immense stones, and wield a club with another, and a sword with a third, while the fourth was poking a long spear at the enemy, and the fifth and sixth were shooting him with a bow and arrow. But luckily, though the giants were so huge and had so many arms, they had each but one heart, and that no bigger or braver than the heart of an ordinary man. . . .

Confronted with all this:

"I must encounter the peril," answered Jason, composedly, "since it stands in the way of my purpose."

It may seem a long jump from Argos to Cotton Junction, Georgia, and young Queenie Peavie in Robert Burch's story, with the responsibility of doing something about her life dropped squarely in her own lap, but it may be in stories like these that a child can most clearly glimpse the hero in himself.

She (Queenie) smiled when she realized what a lecture she had given herself. "I preached myself a sermon," she thought, "and the good part of it was . . . I listened."

A child can measure himself against the heroes in the stories of Hans Christian Andersen and find, many years later, that they are still with him. These stories, which often synthesize several folktales with simpler plots into one, are ageless. The stakes of their heroism are high; the moral choices are serious; the conflicts and the rueful humor that makes the conflicts bearable are those of life.

A princess well could grieve:

An honest prince you rejected. The rose and the nightingale were not to your taste. But the swineherd—you could kiss him for the sake of a musical box. Now you can have what you asked for!

51

And with that he went into his kingdom, shut the door and bolted it; but she could stand outside if she cared to and sing:
"Ah, my dear Augustine,
Our dreams are all done, done, done!"

In the barnyard:

"What pretty children you have, my dear!" said the old duck with the rag on her leg."All of them but one, who doesn't seem right. I only wish you could make him all over again."

Later a hen gives advice to the duckling, now a fledgling swan:

"You may take my word for it—if I say unpleasant things to you, it's all for your own good; that's just how you can tell which are your real friends. Only see that you lay eggs and learn how to purr or give out sparks!"

For Andersen had seen men reject the songs of nightingales for the tinkle of baubles. He had seen hearts like Kay's, chilled in the frosts of Reason, trying in vain to create an *eternity* from patterns, when only human warmth and love would make the patterns come right.

Through tests by water and fire the steadfast tin soldier remains upright.

"On, on, brave warrior!
On, where death awaits thee!"

Eyes open to his fate, knowing all the odds, it never occurred to him to flinch or falter in his devotion to the little dancer. A toy? Only on the surface.

Even a young child responds to a heroism less obvious than

that of knights and warriors—a heroism that is inner rather than outer.

How often the poignancy of a stilled tongue, when one has so much to tell, occurs in the tales of Andersen, a poet who kept many of his deepest feelings to himself.

In November 1962, I went to Hawaii as guest of the Honolulu Book Fair. A few days before I left New York I reread *The Wild Swans*. All the blandishments of Hawaii and of the people I met there could not erase the powerful images of that story from my mind. When I flew from one island to another, I saw the shadow of the plane on the clouds below as that of Elisa borne aloft in the net by her wild swan brothers. When on Thanksgiving Day I saw with a friend the great waves crashing in at Sunset Beach, I thought of the waves that gave her courage to be inexhaustible in her search for her brothers. *The Wild Swans* is a story from Andersen's maturity—a story of longing, terror, and steadfastness of spirit. The images of nature make bearable that longing.

It is a story of contrasts of light and shade, and so I tried to picture it—in dragged pen line and ink and rubbed color. Distant perspectives seen from the eyes of great swans in flight—and the pain of looking closely, in enforced silence, on those one loves most. But dark toads turn into bright poppies when they touch the innocent Elisa; the darkest part of the forest, that is deepest despair, opens up to the vast, open spaces of the sea:

It keeps rolling on, untiring, and that is how it shapes the hard things smooth, and I will be as untiring as it is.

The dark waves rear up in white crests; a white swan swoops over the dark vault of Elisa's prison. Over the dark tumbrel, with a flashing and beating of wings, the swans descend; a white flower blooms like a star on the pile of faggots, and the story ends in a dazzle of release and light.

So much of living swings between the extremes of dark and light. The most honest books we can give our children do not tarnish the dazzle by obliterating the gloom. Banish pain, hurt, controversy from a child's book and you damage the child's capacity to empathize and endure and cope with them.

The art of making books for children cannot be quite so free as that of the painter. When I work, I feel on me the eyes of the children to whom I have told stories. But an author-illustrator submits his craft and himself to an end—the idea of his book. The real moral he puts into it will be the spiritual aura that he has had with him all the years before he wrote it. It will show through writing and pictures, and there doesn't seem to be much he can do about it. Illustration and text—only together do they form the amalgam that is the complete expression of the book. For adults, each line, color, and shape will set associations in motion. For the child, the lines, colors, and shapes he sees are creating his fund of associations—he is so brand-new.

Who forces analysis of this amalgam on a little child can narrow the range of his marvelous imagination, can limit to the rational the use of his otherwise intuitive mind.

Would we see those five gallant Chinese brothers, little Tim, Andy, and Madeline—and Petunia with her legs in the air—laid out in the cold mortuary of forgetfulness, along with so many of Shakespeare's characters, killed forever for young readers by too much analysis too soon?

To break down the parts of a work of art or of a book with young children, to force them to give out too much in reaction, may indicate that we don't trust a book's way with a child. It may be the adult who cannot feel the book. Too insistent techniques that obliterate the spirit of a text in visual noisiness and that distort the proportion of one part to another cannot serve a book well. After the first bedazzzlement, calculated and contrived books will be silent in their barrenness. Spirit will speak from where it dwells. And it is spirit that will lead a child in his struggle to be human.

A young person's heroism may consist in pushing himself beyond the limits set for him by his society, his class, his race. For land, race, class mean nothing so much as being human.

As a child reads of the Finnish heroes from the *Kalevala* in Babette Deutsch's telling, he will feel the spirit of a proud people, with its wealth forged in vessels of gold, or silver, or copper—a people that sang.

In those days, when the world was new and cold, the power of a man lay not only in the strength of his arms. He must also have knowledge of many things and a fine voice. For to know the names of things and to sing well was a way of making magic. . . .

A hero boasts before he meets the mighty singer Vainamoinen:

I will sing my own songs. I will sing him into stone shoes. I will sing him into wooden trousers. I will sing a rock onto his shoulders and a stone onto his heart. I will sing his hands into stone gloves and his head into a helmet of stone.

The child will feel the joy and lusty strength of the life force in Vainamoinen, who, with his brother Ilmarin, the smith— who forged the heavens and welded the arch of the air— restored the natural rhythm of day and night, summer and winter, to the earth. The book ends with a chant of creation and the farewell of Vainamoinen—and perhaps of the age of myth.

None knows where he sailed or whether he will return. None has heard since the pure strains of his kantele. But parts of his songs are remembered, and sung even now, and most of them you have heard, and the few remaining, if you are eager for them, it may be that one day you shall yet hear.

And the book carries the reader out of its own time into timelessness.

In folk legend, history of real men and fancy become mixed in memory—witness the stories of William Tell, Dick Whittington, Davy Crockett, or George Washington. The folk or legendary hero dwarfs life because he embodies the ideals and aspirations of a whole people. To the facts, and the tales told and embroidered in the telling, each age adds its own virtues and paraphernalia. What comes down to us is often a tale of Man rather than of a man.

If a tale pleased—and the singer was gifted—who would question its factual truth? There are other kinds. For song was to many peoples what it was to the ancient Mayas—a symbol of creative life.

A sweet-voiced flower is my mind,
A sweet-voiced flower is my drum. . . .

And so the chant of the ancient Hawaiians—flower of mind, flower of sensuous feeling for beauty, and witness to the mystical union of man with the phenomena of nature.

The images of grandeur to the Hawaiians were the plumes of mountain birds, storm clouds over basalt cliffs, rearing crests of the huge waves from the great ocean. In a land without metallic ores, without the usual crafted trappings of splendor, splendor stood in the glance and stance of a man.

At the end of my first trip to Hawaii, I was given a collection of legends. One story interested me particularly, "The Story of Paka'a and His Son Ku," a story of one boy's thrust beyond his age into an adult world of wounded feelings and revenge, beyond the mores of his own culture toward more humanity. I felt it might have something to say to boys and girls today. So I returned to Hawaii and returned again to see if I could absorb the atmosphere of that legend, possibly based in part on fact, since the king, Keawe-nui-a-'Umi, once lived.

It is a legend from an apparently primitive people—not the noble savages idealized by the escapists from crowded urban centers, but a people with an oral history, with long migrations and echoes of ancient civilizations in its past, in its poetry, in its dance, in its bones. A legend of the sea—raiser of questions, and in its vast depths often the final answer; a legend of the poignancy of island dwellers, whose greeting is pregnant with farewell; a legend of a boy's struggle to find himself and his place in his own world. For Ku is always becoming. With each growth he becomes more and more himself and more and more the racial ideal of the young noble, to whom audacity, the breaking of taboos, power over the wind and waves are natural and permitted.

In the story of Paka'a and Ku those of us far off in time and space can hear the sea surge through our own past. In Ku's groping to think beyond his own time and people, we can feel the challenge and question of the future.

Youth sometimes fears commitments, gifts of the self, which if betrayed, damage whole areas of the psyche. And yet something tells them and us that what was feared, that final gift of one's spirit, the total risk of oneself, is a key that will unlock life to them, will reveal the hero within.

MY GOALS AS AN ILLUSTRATOR

"Each artist has his own way of working. After awhile, he works in possibly the only way he can, given his own temperament."

When recently I was invited to speak on my goals as an illustrator, I was reminded that twenty years ago I was asked to give a talk and write a paper on this same subject. As I reread that paper, I saw that most of my ideas have not changed very much but have only become more pronounced. Just as when one watches landscape the distant things stay put while those nearby are changing constantly, so one's goals in illustration do not change often enough to provide good ammunition for the speeches illustrators are asked to make about their work.

Often reactions to performance in one of the arts will reveal something about another. A few evenings ago a friend and I heard and saw a performance of *Oedipus Rex* by Stravinsky, a modern musical score based on the classical theme and nour-

A speech given at a symposium on Design and Illustration in Children's Books at the University of California, Berkeley, Calif., July 1966. Published in *The Horn Book,* June 1967.

ished in its composing by many heroic examples for voice and instruments from other periods. The "visual presentation" had been entrusted to a painter of considerable reputation who saw fit to vie with the composer for honors in creating a parallel composition of the costumes and décor. He used a prizefight, with Oedipus the popular hero, in the usual satin bathrobe and prizefighter's shoes, in an effort to bring the ancient conflict of Oedipus into a modern arena, where it might appear to be more meaningful than in its own period. What was forgotten was the idea that the story so transcends its period, and evidently any treatment of it, that the attempt to pin it to the present seemed ludicrous. The thing did not come off. One wondered why there had been such a lack of faith in the work itself, which needed no help from anyone, and lack of faith in the audience.

I often think of illustrators as I think of performers of music. Those one can listen to longest are often those most selfless, those who are content to be a medium for the music. They put their own individualities at the service of the music to probe its depths and reveal its spirit, rather than to display the idiosyncracies of their own personalities. Techniques that hammer can dull the eyes as well as the ears.

Even though I may be the composer, I have come to think of the illustrator more and more as the performer of the spirit of a book. If one lives with a book from its beginning, one may be closer to that spirit. Some spirits speak so loudly their voices are unmistakable. Others are more delicate. No one way can be called the best way to interpret them to a child.

Feelings appropriate to the fine arts, especially painting, are often called forward in speaking about illustration for children. Little children readily look at all kinds and styles of art. They are probably the freest and most imaginative audience in the world. But illustration is illustration and not painting. It is communication of the idea of a book.

This all sounds obvious and has been said many times before. But every book I illustrate has to be considered in these terms.

By now most of us realize that ours is an age in transition, an age in which many old values are being turned upside down and many old solutions are no longer valid. We love dramatic descriptions of phenomena, but the word *explosion* is not too violent a one to describe the swift changes we are undergoing.

In a delightful Italian picture book, *nella notte buia,* Bruno Munari shows a little cat that sees a light in the sky, far off. He goes to find his little friend, and they hold a conversation on a bench in the black space of night, with the little light far off in the sky. Their paws are around each other's necks and their tails are entwined.

"Do you like little white mice?"

A bat flies overhead, and of course the cats are afraid. One runs off; the other takes refuge under a flower in a pot until the bat, too, grows smaller and smaller in the distance. Meanwhile the light still shines.

But a little boy and his father are not content just to watch the light from below. They bring a ladder. "Let's go see," says the little boy. Another man appears with his ladder. They make a little structure, and one of the men, with valor and a certain flair to his gestures, starts to climb up. Another man appears with his ladder, and there develops a most interesting balancing act, with appropriate display of masculine bravery, skill, and vigor. The little boy seems to be ballast for one end of the lowest ladder. Then still a fourth man shows up with his ladder.

The last picture in the episode shows men, hats, ladders flying through the air, topsy-turvy. One man is trying to make off with the longest ladder. But on the end of it is the little cat, who had just been out to enjoy the evening, gaily riding through the air. And the episode ends, showing the source of the light: "And here is the firefly that is going to sleep in the field because by now it is day."

And so with delicacy of feeling, with very few lines, and almost as few words, an artist who is also a poet makes a comment on how things are.

One wonders if that little cat is not very much like the child of today, riding out chaos and explosions, while someone is trying to make off with the big end of the ladder.

Twenty years ago bookmaking still struggled under wartime restrictions, but there were the examples of excellence from the twenties and thirties to look up and back to: *The White Cat* by Elizabeth MacKinstry (1928); *Millions of Cats* by Wanda Gág (1928); *The Painted Pig* by René d'Harnoncourt (1930); *The Fairy Circus* by Dorothy Lathrop (1931); *Calico Bush* by Rachel Field (1931); *Ola* by the d'Aulaires (1932); *Andy and the Lion* by James Daugherty (1938); *Mei Li* by Thomas Handforth (1938). But at the same time the field was plagued with books that had the saccharinity of greeting cards, books that possibly filled some emotional need and were very successful commercially but which did not even attempt to give a child an honest picture of himself or life around him.

Many artists pleaded with those working with children to be more open to experimental illustration and to work derived from contemporary painting, and to raise their personal standards of taste. Much more interest began to focus on the individual author and artist and his contribution.

Here we are, twenty years later, trying to ride out the explosions, like that little cat that only came to admire the light on a summer night.

To serve the huge numbers of today's children about seventy publishers are putting out nearly three thousand books each year. Houses that had one editor, who often handled all promotion as well as editing (one even wrapped up the books), and one secretary in the juvenile department now have several to many editors and assistants.

Twenty years ago we were pleading for more receptivity to the new. Now we can ask ourselves to take a long look at the guests we have so blithely invited in.

As foreign-born artists have been more and more absorbed into the American scene, national contributions to American illustration from other countries have diminished. Many publishers reprint translations of foreign picture books, just as other countries reprint some of ours in order to enrich their own lists. Commercial techniques are now exchanged so widely internationally that it is a bit hard to identify the individual contributions of a particular country. Many artists have come to the field of illustration from that of painting or printmaking and have brought great richness of technical experience as well as personal freedom to their work.

Today a sculptor can fashion clean rectangular boxes, or give an order to a cabinetmaker to fashion them, and announce that his work is signing the death warrant of all previous art. And the announcement is listened to and taken seriously. Critics write enthusiastically about shows of optical experiments that used to be part of a design student's art-school training. The latest fads from a fashionable art market are put forth for a child's consumption a few months after a brief foray in the advertising field. Many books seem to be put out for oversized children in adult skins. The huge and overwhelming single image on a page, when the object described is only an incidental detail in the story; the indiscriminate use of close and hot color harmonies derived from the fashion world; overblown illustrations in overblown color in which the thread of a story or fable is lost in the extravagant garment given it—these are in the books that are not content to persuade but scream for attention and all too clearly proclaim their origin in a highly competitive market.

Speaking of a complex contemporary musical score of more visual than audible interest, Harold Schonberg, music critic of *The New York Times,* wrote of "Decibel Power versus Expressive Power." They are not the same. We could describe such books of decibel power as books for the eye (often of enormous visual interest as objects) instead of books for the eye and mind and heart, in which the whole book and each of its parts function to express in just proportion the idea within. Many people have confounded the aims and methods of illustration with those of fine art, which has its origin in an entirely different level of the unconscious. They forget that a book starts with an idea, whether or not it has a text, and illustration is at its service. Successful illustration extends, embellishes, illuminates, but never obliterates the idea.

In spite of the dashing compositions, the blowups, the typographical shocks, many of our books today are conventional. Each age sets up its own conventions. One has only to look at publishers' catalogues to see some of ours: The children who seem to call to the reader, "Look, Ma, I'm acting!" instead of going about their own business; the stereotypes of harebrained but charming elderly friends of children; the mechanical abstractions of trees and animals; the orange-pink color schemes, no matter what the subject; the huge blown-up image from contemporary poster technique, with the main interest in design; neo-Victorianism in fine pen-line techniques derived from ninteenth-century engravings and drawings; delicate and poetic ideas awash in a sea of textures and colors that all but drown them, that stultify and limit a child's response; use of collage and mixed media—such as crayon and woodcut—together, occasionally at the price of the graphic unity of the page; visual elements from other works that had a deeper origin in reaction to life—tag ends of art techniques filtered down from painting, through commercial illustration, finally to become manner and formula in the child's book; morbidity of technique—tattered rags and incrustations of decay that come from painting techniques. What do they have to say to a child, unless the decay is purposeful, a part of the story being told?

If my mentioning these trends, which can so often result in visual clichés (but which need *not* if the idea of the book remains uppermost in importance), seems negative, perhaps it is because we become so accustomed to virtues in what is close to us that we hardly notice them and are roused only by apparent faults.

Never before have illustrators been so sure of a welcome for their most extravagant and bizarre experiments. Never has such lavish production been put at the disposal of the little child's picture book. The barker's voice in the marketplace must be loud to be heard and his wares must glitter.

When experimentation and breaking down the visual means into their simplest elements occur at the total service of the idea, we can get something as imaginative as Leo Lionni's *Little Blue and Little Yellow.* Collage can be used to tell the story richly, with the textures employed adding a dimension of visual metaphor to the story, as in the same artist's *Inch by Inch.*

Artists are constantly enlarging their fund of means to tell a story. We can ask that the means remain means, that experimentation and techniques remain tools, not ends. The search for novelty can be our goal; it can also be our curse.

Some artists, like Maurice Sendak in much of his recent work, are harking back with wit and re-creation of atmosphere to some of the best of the nineteenth-century line illustrators—Cruikshank, Tenniel, and Richard Doyle—and are performing a most valuable service in revitalizing a tradition that is probably much more vigorous than many of our seductive eye-catchers that remain on the decorative level and hardly attempt to illustrate a story in depth.

There seems to be very great interest in the composing process, in the *how* of making a book. It might be a good idea if we were occasionally to ask *why*, and we might end up with "Why on earth?" There is a great interest in the contribution of the individual artist, but perhaps we are asking him to talk too much about how he works and are not looking hard enough at what he does.

Some time ago I was one of probably a great many people who received a questionnaire from the National Council of Teachers of English on the "composing process"—as good a name as any for it—to try to track down what is elusive in the process of making books. The questions were intelligently thought out, as such things go. But I suspect that what is elusive will remain so, since it is a subtle combination of personality, inner drive, and imagination in the author or illustrator himself.

Illustration and writing are often a lonely business, and artists when they get together often compare notes on ways of working. I am often asked why each of my books is apt to look different from the others. Each artist has his own way of working. After a while he works in possibly the only way he can, given his own temperament. I feel about each book very differently. My interest is in the book as a whole, not just in the illustrations. Every detail of a book should, as far as possible, reflect the intention the artist and designer had toward the idea of the book. These intentions need not even be expressible in words, but they should be felt. That quality of the individual book that is strongest—the simple vigor, the delicacy, the mood, the setting—should determine the color, not an arbitrary application of brilliance to whatever the subject.

The atmosphere of a book is extremely important; in older boys' and girls' books it is perhaps more important than depiction of events. A story that is very traditional in feeling can often suffer from illustrations that are stylistically too different in period. When one adapts a modern technique to illustrations for a historical period, one must think of the young child looking, with little knowledge of period. Do the costumes give the feeling of the period if they do not reproduce the details?

Freshness lies in the intensity of expression, not in the novelty of the technique.

In order not to drag the ideas or techniques that I have developed during work on one book into another, I try to take a good piece of time between books, painting or just taking in impressions by travel, in order to clear the way for the next.

Some books are of course related by period, and the same research holds for both; this is true of *Cinderella* and *Puss in Boots*. But the spirit of the two is completely different. The quality in a story itself and in the way it is told determines style. Puss is extravagant, swaggering. The king, a *bon viveur,* enjoys the outrageousness of the cat. *Cinderella,* with the tenderness of the godmother, the dream of the girl, the preposterousness of the sisters, is in a completely different mood.

People speak of some artists who use different techniques as if they had fifty up their sleeves ready to appear, fullblown, when needed. But the life of an artist is one of constant preparation. He almost never feels that he has realized his aim.

When a book is finished, he is usually just beginning to feel how it might have been. Stacks of trial drawings and rejects attest to many efforts to find the right way to say what one has to say. One develops the technique necessary to express one's feeling about the particular book in hand. Sometimes this takes several months of drawing into a subject until one is ready to begin the actual illustrations.

People often ask how much time it takes to make a book. Five days, five months, three years—as long as is necessary to get down one's ideas and feelings about the book.

It might be useful for me to tell you of my work on three different books, each of which presented a different problem in illustration and bookmaking. They happen to be mine, and I use them because I know them best.

One is a picture book, one a picture-story book, and one an illustrated book for older children. All three are of folk origin: One is a fable, one of the oldest types of folktales; one is a synthesis of several European folktales through a poet's mind; one is a hero legend with chants from a people with an oral culture.

Myths and legends tell a child who he is in the family of man. In a book with ancient, mythic origins, some of the poetic depth of the story should be implied in the illustrations. The child, looking and reading, will understand and recall tomorrow more than he can tell you today.

Once a Mouse . . . is a picture book in which the pictures complete a very brief text and, I hope, add some comment of their own. Since the book is for very young children, the details are only those needed. The woodcut is a favorite medium of mine, one that relates to traditional graphic media and that can be very successfully combined with type on a page.

Though the words of the fable are few, the theme is big. It

takes a certain amount of force to cut a wooden plank, and a definite decision. Wood that lived can say something about life in a forest. An artist can make his own color proofs in print-ers' inks, can mix his colors and give an approximate formula to a printer. Even though the transparent colors on an offset press are different from the thicker ones used at home, this proving can be of enormous help in seeing what one will get.

Each artist has his personal feelings about his way of work-ing, and the finished book is what is to be judged as successful or not, but in my own books I like every color to be cut on a separate block in order to maintain the optical unity of the medium. A book is like a very small stage. Just as a violent drama on television is sometimes hard to take in one's living room, what is effective in a large print can often break up a comparatively small book page.

The story of *Once a Mouse* . . . moves in an arc from qui-etness to quietness; from meditation, to concern, to involve-ment, to anger and action, back to meditation. The colors I chose were the yellow-green of sun through leaves, of earth, the dark green of shadows, and the red that says India to me. Red is used as a force to cut into the other colors when its violence is needed. Excitements are fairly easy to make in illustrations—a chase, a fight, an explosion—and offer imme-diate release. The quiet power of inner life is much harder to achieve and must be felt more deeply.

Just before I went to Hawaii in 1962 I had reread *The Wild Swans* of Andersen. There are vast images in that story, vast implications and sonorities that can ring in a child's mind far into adult life. It is a story with strong contrasts: dark toads and bright poppies; the forest pool in its shadow and the shimmer of light through the leaves; the darkest part of the forest—no bird was seen, no sunbeam pierced the bloom—"yes, indeed, there was solitude here, the like of which she had never known." And then the free, vast spaces of the sea, the dark waves rearing up to show their white sides.

Between the black cypresses that would be there in an Italian graveyard shines the moon. Over the tumbrel bearing Elisa to her death the eleven swans descend, and the story ends with the miracle of the white flower in a dazzle of light and happiness.

To try to show these contrasts I used a broad lettering pen dragged over rough watercolor paper and sumi for the gray washes. I needed the simplest means of achieving dark and light. The rose color for the swans' beaks, for the dawn, for the poppies and the roses I got from rubbing sanguine powder into the plastic contact plate. I was afraid to trust delicate washes either to dropout halftone or hand-clearing. The drawings were frequently vignetted around the type to tie the two more intimately together and to give variety to the movement of the book.

When I was in Hawaii I was so enchanted with the natural beauty of the islands and the charm of the people, I did not even think of looking for material for a book. The Hawaiian folklore I knew was long, involved, and difficult for a Western child. And the wild swans had ensnared me for most of the winter and spring following that first visit.

But just before I left the islands, an elderly lady gave me a historic collection of legends gathered by her husband's uncle, who had grown up on the island of Kaua'i. One story interested me particularly, "The Story of Paka'a and His Son Ku." After the swans were in flight, I decided to return to Hawaii to see if I could get inside the atmosphere enough to do a book for children based on that legend, full of racial memories of the people, also full of courage, of a boy's struggle to find himself, to discover his own place, to leap, at least in thought, beyond the mores of his own culture. The leap beyond the usual, the accepted, is so often what defines the folk hero. His audacity embodies the longings of a people for something beyond—beyond the next promontory, beyond the blue-black water where the sharks dwell, beyond the next island, beyond a restrictive social structure controlled by taboos. The material thrilled me, and I went into it more deeply, reading in Polynesian and Hawaiian myths and anthropological studies, talking to proud people who retained after 150 years of foreign influence some of the old thought patterns and ideals of their fathers.

Dorothy Kahananui, Hawaiian musician and professor of Hawaiian at the University, led me to a full Hawaiian version of the legend, containing the old chants—so significant a part of Hawaiian life—the most important tie of knowledge and feeling of the past to the present and essential to the atmosphere and telling of the story. She agreed to make a literal translation for me, and I worked out my own version from that and from the two other versions that exist in English.

While I was writing the story of Paka'a, which swings back and forth from the delineation of character to the natural phenomena that form character and provide images of magnificence to describe it, I was natually thinking of the illustrations. Full color would not only have been out of the question in cost for a long book for older children but would have intruded too insistently on a story that is one of internal struggle and growth as well as external action.

Except for enigmatical pictographs, of great interest to anthropologists but very primitive graphically, and wood and stone images of gods, there was almost no Hawaiian art that seemed effective to me as inspiration for illustrations for a legend for young people with probably a vague picture of a tourist's paradise. I had thought of a carved medium, woodcut or linoleum, one that might hark back to the elegantly simple carvings and also one that could depict the atmosphere in which such legends arose. I finally settled on linoleum, and two points of view evolved in the illustrations that are also in my telling of the story. One is the background of vast natural forces—the winds that were thought to bear the tales; the basalt cliffs that gave an ideal to men's character; the vast spaces of the sea, source of life and food, testing ground of prowess, image of both beauty and poignant and unfulfilled longing. The other is a simple delineation of character, pared down to its essence in the most direct of emotional confrontations. Linoleum, which can be cut or engraved, seemed to be the answer.

The color I chose for the printing was close to that I recall most strongly when I think of Hawaii—the deep green of the clefts in the great palis, where all softness has worn away in wind and rain but where living plants have clad the cliffs in velvet. I chose a deep, warm, almost olive green to harmonize with the warm-toned paper.

Margaret Evans, who designed the typography, chose Palatino, a type that has the strength and individuality in its cut to halt the eye on the individual word. I had tried to tell the story with strong, simple words, most of them Anglo–Saxon, words of action, with metaphors taken from Hawaiian life. The pictures would have to reflect the feelings of those words. Big things had to remain big. Action should have meaning, but thought and inner feeling are also action in illustration. I found this illustration for older children a challenge, with a more rigid type page than that of the picture book, with a very different mental approach from the reader.

The title page is symbolic—the steering paddle that meant comand; the kahili, the feather standard, that meant royalty and the watchful care of a backbone for his king; the cliff that meant the rock-heart that does not yield or wear away. A windy book from a windy land.

In *The Little Prince,* Saint-Exupéry makes a statement in the context of one human relationship that perhaps we could apply to another: "One is forever responsible for whom one has tamed." Children walk, arms open, to embrace what we give them. To hand on to them the breakdown in comunication that is all around us is a very serious thing. Those who work with children should be encouraged to hand on to them their personal involvement with the world. A child needs the stimulus of books that are focused on individuality in personality and character if he is to find his own. A child is individual; a book is individual. Each should be served according to its needs.

ALICE DALGLIESH

On a hill on the side of a Connecticut ridge looking off to the west over the Housatonic valley is a solid, cozy little house nestled into the earth. A hayfield stretches above it over the hill, a thicket of pines lies to one side, maples give shade and homes to birds, lilacs bloom by the door, forsythia gilds a soft red barn in the spring. Here Alice Dalgliesh makes her home with her friend Margaret Evans, former art editor of Scribners.

The first time I saw Alice Dalgliesh was in the Central Children's Room of the New York Public Library, where I was an assistant. Her novel for young people, *The Silver Pencil* (Scribners), based on her childhood in Trinidad, her school days in England, and her early years of teaching, had just been published. She told of her father's gift of the silver pencil, a challenge to the imaginative child who was already finding satisfaction in writing, and a trust for the future, for her father died when she was ten, and she was to take up his challenge early.

For me, Alice's real setting was not the office of Books for Young Readers at Charles Scribner's Sons, where I took my own books to her as editor, but that simple old Connecticut saltbox where I have known her as friend. Many times I was a

---

Published by the Children's Book Council in *The Calendar,* January 1972.

guest in the apartment-studio—with a huge weeping willow near the door. The house, a solid bulwark against the force of cold New England winters and hot and thunderous summers, seems so much an extension of Alice that it is hard for me to imagine previous owners, although they left their marks: the transformation of the barn, with its huge window looking out over the lush valley, the great andirons for the huge old central fireplace that had been forged from pieces of girders left from the construction of the George Washington Bridge, the strength of the solid hewn beams and floorboards from trees thicker than most you see now in the second-growth forests of the area.

The containment of all details in almost stark simplicity, the warmth of the fieldstone fireplace and the flags of the hearth, big as an apartment kitchen, the harmony of simple old furniture, hunted down and upholstered with coverings so carefully chosen that they seem to have grown on it, the solid and gay Quimper pottery, opulent bouquets of flowers, arranged in the hand as she picked them, with the intense love of and feeling for harmonious color that prompted her to try barn paint mixtures for several weeks until she got the soft red she wanted, shelves crammed full of books, pictures from illustrator friends, a hooked rug made by Rachel Field, recalling happy summers at Sandy Cove in Nova Scotia—all these tell much about the person as well as her craft. Much of my own feeling for that part of Connecticut where I now make my home came from those visits with Alice in Brookfield. After my long hours of working on the linoleum cuts for *Dick Whittington* (Scribners) on the old caramel-colored tilt-top table in the barn, we would explore seemingly endless delightful little roads through woods, by tumbling streams, coming upon vistas over miles of layers of blue hills. Just as Alice as an editor might have had as her motto "Once accepted, forever loved," so she had come to love Connecticut like a convert. Her American citizenship has been and is to her a privilege fiercely and proudly defended. There is the same involvement with the destiny of a book or of a place. She is endlessly curious about the character of the sturdy early settlers of Connecticut, like the family of Sarah Noble, as well as the friendly Indians who had not had to hate whom they did not fear. We explored settings of local Indian legends of Chief Waramaug and campaigns of the Revolution that lived again in *Adam and the Golden Cock* (Scribners). Much that harks back to England in Connecticut—place names, a skin of reserve over inner warmth, similarity of leafy landscapes, an individuality in people nurtured by an affectionate tolerence of eccentricity— would make the child of English parents feel at home.

Alice told me much of her childhood at San Fernando—the enchanted afternoons flying kites in Paradise Gardens, with childhood's ignoring of the racial barriers adults respected. Like the memory of that hot tropical sun that warmed the pale gold and blue child, the warmth of heart of the New Englander expresses itself in unusual feeling for the individuality and needs of young children, the warmth of the teacher informing the editor and guiding the author. Alice has delighted in the friendships of a procession of children throughout her life — those she taught, those of friends, relatives and neighbors, and those she has brought back to rich life from legends and history's spare records.

The sturdy saltbox has sheltered many, many friends who have shared its warmth — Dola de Jong, Katherine Milhous, Genevieve and Joanna Foster, Hildegarde Woodward, Leonard Weisgard. . . . Alice and Margaret now spend winters in Woodbury, where the driveway in winter is more nearly horizontal, but as soon as spring really means business, they are back at the saltbox in Brookfield.

A LOOK AT TIDE POOLS

"The tide flows in and out, and the child gathers the colored fragments, and some he keeps. What will the next tide bring?"

The other day I stood on a rocky outcropping at the ocean's edge, mesmerized by the ceaseless ebb and flow of the teeming life in the tide pools. These small worlds seem almost complete unto themselves and protected from the currents of the open water; yet each new wave sends kelp, crabs, urchins, snails topsy-turvy, and the whole look changes. Brown, encrusted crabs that a moment before seemed stones scuttle sidewise to a new cover. Little coiled snail shells that seemed empty and dead suddenly sprout tiny horns and begin to search the pebbly floor. Sweeps of kelp fold back on themsleves and relax in new flowerings. Ropelike forms snake their way along a current, only to form new knots and macramé in the backwash.

The world of children's book illustration sometimes seems just such a little pool, subject to its own currents and laws, yet utterly sensitive to every wash and current from the outer flood. Some solid old stones stay fixed, glistening in occa-

Published in *Publishers Weekly*, July 15, 1974, as "The Shifting Tides of Children's Illustration."

sional sun and dour and gray in cloud. Some slow snails leave the only discernible tracks left on the sand after all the flower-like explosions of kelp have subsided and dried. A field that is rich with life one minute can dry to a tangle of old lines, shoe-laces, and twisted papers the next—until revitalized a few hours later by the fresh sweep of incoming currents.

Today must be a marvelous time for a young artist to enter the field of children's book illustration. He steps into a teem-ing, restless world, fortunate in that his nostalgia for his own childhood can serve as both memory and guide, warmed by the sun of old struggles won, and probably more free than his crusty, barnacled forebears could hope to be. To hold his own in the restless swarm around him, he needs a strong sense of personal direction, a reliance on his own strengths and indi-viduality. The more clearly he sees himself, the more personal will be his work. He will be spread naked as a specimen for dissection on the pages of his printed work, subject to the sometimes weary, sometimes eager eyes of critics and children.

The old survival laws are very active in tide pools. Over-population sickens and suffocates. Tossed-in junk, tin cans, refuse can kill the symbiotic, interacting life system, but the pool is host to them all.

All over the country the Children's Book Showcase, spon-sored by the Children's Book Council, has spawned similar showcases of well-designed and illustrated books. Librarians and teachers know that if they are to offset some of the junk children see, they must point out quality to parents and get the books into the hands of children to make their own way. In this third year of the showcase, all children's artists can be happy that Margot Zemach, a gifted artist with humor and élan, and a superb storyteller in pictures, has won the Calde-cott Medal.

My staring into tide pools is really connected with my embrace of photography as another way of seeing and catching things on the wing. It is a double joy to be able to grasp the moment of vision and then to savor it and muse over it at leisure. Knowing what I can get with a lens pushes me to draw what I cannot.

Those who work with children do not really need to be told that we all absorb more with visual images than without. Cameras now are so good and so available that a way of recording is accessible to many people who never had the time or discipline to learn how to draw. But the eye's selectivity, the spirit and nervous impulse behind the eye, still determines what the image says.

Many artists are copying photographs of action shots of athletes, children in motion, animals that they can hardly hope to find as models. Some have enough life behind their pens to bring the child copied to new life on the page; others simply do not, and we are left with seams in trousers and wrinkles in sleeves instead of a person. The fashion photographer pins the eye-catching stances of his models with a wide-angle lens and a motor-drive. Then fashion drawing takes over the exaggerated look, and soon some child in a book done in Peter Max's technique is wearing shoes size 17. Telescopic lenses in the hands of astronauts have shown our world as a luminous, magical sphere. Close-up lenses enable us to get so close to it that we can wander through mosses like the insects we picture, and literally know what Thumbelina saw.

Under the pressure toward "curriculum orientation," publishers have devised new ways to stir the imagination of children with beautifully illustrated informational books, provocative social histories. Some very talented photographers, survivors from the death of the major picture magazines, have turned to children's books and filmstrips. Plants and animals, after all, aren't the only creations to go through metamorphoses. Filmstrips could possibly be books in another form—banal in some hands, a vital new art form in others, stimulating interest in all directions.

Some creatures dig deep in one spot and make secure nests for themselves, others are forever on the move. Maurice Sendak, for instance, has been digging for years into his own psychic roots. And great themes help artists to make great illustrations. The great storytellers—Andersen, Grimm, Perrault—all are palimpsests bearing traces of ancient folk experience. Children sense the mysteries there, I think, and are more magnetized by an honest facing of the implications of such tales than they will tell.

Different pools in the same rock mass attract different creatures to different water levels. Regional publishers, with specialized lists of books about their own locale, have sprung up in many parts of the country, publishing local authors and illustrators with firsthand knowledge of an area. For example, Island Heritage Limited, with editorial offices in Honolulu, is bringing out Hawaiiana in picture books—legends and original material illustrated by artists living in Hawaii. Their work is much closer to Hawaiian fact and spirit than that of many mainland artists who often have a sketchy research background. Some of Island Heritage's reprints of Japanese folk tales, illustrated by Japanese illustrators, have the immediacy and gusto of Samurai films.

And there are always new colors in the pool. Many young people now are turning to art as a way of life, and their nostalgic posters of Art Nouveau, the thriftshop laces and boas, turn up in intricate collages of textures. Old catalogue cuts in the public domain appear now in striking new combinations with new meanings. We are in a period of brilliant political caricature and cartoons, of collages often with surreal overtones.

Rising costs of color reproduction have necessitated the use of black-and-white line reproduction. Did the need create the technical pens that make possible such intricately hatched work? The freedom of line possible with these pens can set loose an avalanche of detail in a cathedral being constructed, in a way probably never shown to children before. Hardly a subject is now taboo. Almost as if in answer to the call, a whole group of gifted artists have quietly taken over the field of fine draughtsmanship and have made their pen-and-ink work almost their trademark: Rick Schreiter with Hogarthian exuberance, Tomi Ungerer with a mixture of the innocence, sophistication, and wild absurdity of a René Clair film, Jose Aruego with sure wit.

Woodcutting continues to fascinate and challenge artists, some in broad, simple pictures for very young children, some in intricate evocations of African tribal designs, some in combinations with cut paper and line.

As if to capture better a watery world, transparent watercolor has returned to popularity, with a new look at the old English method of transparent washes by Donald Carrick and Irene Haas, or applied to drawings sinuous as a vine's tendrils, in the style of a century later. Beatrix Potter lives on in the spirit of countless imitators of her animal miniatures.

The tide flows in and out, and the child gathers the colored fragments, and some he keeps. What will the next tide bring?

THE SOUND OF WATER

"Myths tell us who we are."

These past weeks I have been listening to the Senate hearings on the radio in my studio, every once in a while, when the temperature and the decibels rose, running into the other room to have a look at those revealing and concealing faces.

In fact, I could have called this "Wood blocks and Watergate"—the story of my life right now. Every time I hear the word, a most beautiful image of a Chinese moon gate, reflected in water, comes to mind. That's not the same thing at all!

While I was listening, I was also cutting the wood blocks for a picture book for very small children. After working in a meticulous medium, such as the fine-line pen-and-ink drawings that I used to express the crystalline delicacy of *The Snow Queen,* I like to change gears, do something with a completely different feeling. Point of view comes through, no matter what the medium chosen to express the individual feeling one has for a specific book. Past solutions solved past problems, and the pleasures of working on a new book involve risk as soon as one plunges into the work.

A speech given at the Sixth Loughborough Conference in Towson, Md., August 1973.

It is seductive to daydream, but too-prolonged daydreaming can ruin your chances for doing a book, because you complete the idea in your mind—or you think you do—and then you discard it, as you mentally discard all your past work to free yourself for the new. That interval just before beginning actual work, when only belief in what you want to do with the book supports you, is possibly the most precarious of all. As Willa Cather said, "The mind is at bay before the idea." Once you are in, you begin to draw on all kinds of skills, memories, visual metaphors, nervous adjustments, and what individuality you have in your work shows up.

In the book I am working on are many images from our life in the Connecticut woods, especially the butterflies: the first spring azures, like fluttering violets, the sooty swallowtails we saw drying their wings by a pond edge on a May morning, the brown-ash wood moths of summer evenings. Why wood blocks for butterflies? A concentrated fable like *Once A Mouse . . .* might gain force in the telling from the force in the cutting, the challenge of trying to convey some of a jungle's gold and gloom in three colors. But butterflies? Butterflies flutter through this book as a leitmotif, tying together the separate ideas and few words. They will be quite a challenge.

Woodcutting is enormously satisfying work. I sketch directly on the pine blocks in charcoal, trying out compositions with a mirror over my workbench, making corrections, trying to simplify, to make the design strong and clear, because possibly this book may be some child's first, and it must satisfy that kind of healthy sensuality of very young children, who gesture with their bodies the gesture on the page, if the feeling gets through to them. I would like it to stretch them a bit—if possible, please them with the kind of direct strength that went into the cuts.

Woodcutting is a sturdy medium for illustration—rough but

strong. The hand printing of the separation prints is a tremendous challenge. There are so many ways one can print the
same blocks. But if something does work, you can't stop. Then
you hear the rattle of toenails on the floor, and a little dog
comes and asks again and again for someone to go out and
play—and you keep right on printing.

I am sure we have all been doing some thinking and strong
feeling these past few weeks, ranging from "Why?" and "Why
not?" to "Go get him!" and "Try to save the pieces!" And as
we look at those young and not-so-young faces brought in by
the distance lenses, we probably ask ourselves, "Where did
the pattern get so mixed up that so many of us hardly know
who we are and what we value?"

It is almost impossible to stop someone who loves to travel
from telling you more than you would really like to know
about where he has been. If he has taken pictures—unless
you have an elastic span of attention or are a camera buff
yourself—God help you. I'll try to be brief in my word
pictures.

I love being on islands, where you are never far from water:
Denmark, with the cool North Sea to the west, the dark green,
moss-edged moats of manors, with the great swans breaking
their white egg shapes on the surface; the wide Pacific of
Hawaii, with its chanting winds and mountainous waves; the
iridescent barcarole of Venetian waters. Water wears grooves
in all of us. But we all know now that there are no islands anymore. The earth is round. From any two points, excavations,
if deep enough and directed toward the center, are bound to
come together.

I would like to tell you of two points on opposite sides of
the earth that I visited this past year. To one I went to try to
find the child behind Hans Christian Andersen, the man,
among the waterways that had shaped so much of his life and

feeling. To the other island I was drawn by the sound of water, and its beauty and harmony have haunted me. I went to both to take pictures.

In the past year, under the guidance of an excellent photographer who is also a dear friend, I have been working—playing?—delighting my soul with photography. An artist's pleasure is in the sheer joy of using his eyes—part of him arrested, if you will, at the stage of wonder, especially if he is photographing nature, part of him trying to fix what time and space snatch so greedily away. ("Look thy last on all things lovely every hour . . ." with de la Mare. *Look again!*)

I used to feel that the only way to anchor a visual experience was to try to draw it. It is still, for me, one of the best ways. The flow of feeling, concentrated observation, the sheer effort to memorize details serve to engrave images on one's consciousness. With more skill, better photographic equipment, endless tries, one also learns to take better pictures. Will this shot be worth a second, or a tenth, look? Will it astonish me? For isn't so often what we seek — and what we would like to give to children—that jerk to attention? To see and feel life? Close-up lenses reveal a whole world one hardly notices with the naked eye. Great adult bodies can shrink to child size in fresh seeing.

A friend, who shares my love for Andersen, and I set out to look for the child the man revealed so poignantly in his stories—the impressions that bit by bit shaped the man and his determination to look on his life as a fairy tale. We drove, took ferries, drove again, and took more ferries to the three large islands of Denmark and Ærø, to the south.

Odense—the house on Monkmill Street (I quote Andersen): "One single little room, nearly all the space filled up with my father's workshop, and the bench where I slept."

"To be born in a duck's nest, in a farmyard, is of no consequence to a bird, if it is hatched from a swan's egg."

The river that flowed through the village and through the child's life: "The regiment to which my father belonged went, however, no farther than Holstein; peace was concluded and the voluntary warrior was soon sitting at his workshop again. . . . He had lost his good health. One morning he awoke in a state of delirium, talking of campaigns and Napoleon. . . . My mother immediately sent me to fetch help—to a so-called 'wise woman,' who lived a couple of miles from Odense. . . . The woman asked me several questions. . . . 'Now go home along the riverbank. If your father is going to die, you will meet his ghost.' "

The boy tried to remember that running water could fend off ghosts and goblins. He also remembered the Monster of the Deep. He raced home.

"On the third evening my father died. His corpse was left lying on the bed, and I slept on the floor with my mother; and a cricket chirped throughout the night. . . .

" 'He is dead already,' my mother called to it. 'You need not call him; the Ice Maiden has taken him.' I understood what she meant. The previous winter when our windows were frozen over, my father had shown us a figure on one of the panes—a maiden stretching out both arms. 'She must have come to fetch me,' he said in fun. . . .

"My mother went out washing, and I sat alone with the little theatre my father had made for me. I made clothes for my puppets and read plays. . . . My parents had moved further up the street, by the Monkmill Gate, and there we had a garden. The path led down to the river behind the Monkmill. . . . When the sluice gates were closed, all the water ran from the river, the fishes splashed about in the puddles that were left, so that I could catch them in my hands, and under the great waterwheels fat water rats came out from the mill to drink. Suddenly the sluice gates were raised, the water rushed down again, foaming and roaring. I splashed back to the bank as quickly as I could.

" . . . I used to stand on one of the big stones which my mother used as a scrubbing board and sing all the songs I knew at the top of my voice. . . . I had been told by an old woman who washed her clothes in the river that the Empire of China was right under Odense River, and that a Chinese prince, one moonlit night as I was sitting there, might dig his way through the earth to us, hear me sing, and take me to his kingdom with him and make me rich and famous. . . . But it was not thus it was to happen, and yet . . . it was to happen."

We saw the swans the boy Hans Christian might have seen as he boarded ship at Nyborg for Copenhagen to leave his childhood behind him. "But when we sailed out into the Great Belt at Nyborg, and the ship carried me away from the island of my birth, I felt I was far out in the wide world."

The island of Fyn is the island of beautiful manor houses —some in old Dutch style—with moats and swans and the dock leaves that once fed the white snails of Glorup. We went south to Fåborg, and from there to the island of Ærø, and came back with our film cans loaded with flowers—the flowers of Egeskov and the wild flowers such as the child Hans Christian might have seen along the road as he trudged with his mother from Odense to Bogense. We reached the western shore of Jutland and the wide North Sea—with Elise searching for her wild swan brothers: "She looked at the countless pebbles lying there on the beach, all of them round from the grinding of water. Glass, iron, stones — everything that was washed up had been shaped by the water, although this was far softer than her delicate hand. 'It never tires of rolling, and in this way it can smooth down what is hard. I will be just as tireless.' "

Using the images of the tales of terror and horror told to him as a child, the poet distilled the stories that enabled faith in life to put evil in its place.

Today we are apt to travel fast, cover too much ground in too short a space in time. How can we relate to, savor, remember, digest all those impressions? How can we ever find answers to all the questions travel raises? Why do the sea-serpent prows of the Viking ships resemble so closely the naga heads one sees in the countries that embraced Buddhism?

One night in 1952, a large Balinese man sat cross-legged on the stage of a New York theatre, his fingers fluttering over the heads of the long drum he held across his knees, his expression rapt in the rhythms and counterrhythms of an ancient melody. Around him on the floor his friends, musicians from his village of Pliatan, sat before their beautifully carved instruments and gongs. The intricate music they made, the sounds as of water dripping off leaves after a sudden shower, the gurgle and spatter of notes, seemed to carry them, too, far away from the slush and smog of a New York winter, back to the curving mirrors of rice paddies and the swift rivulets of their island homeland. The tinkles, the ripplings, the deep bongs of the gamelan, the exquisite little girl dancers, like tiny gilded dragonflies, darting, weaving, bending to the mesmerizing music, the sweetness of the expressions on the musicians' faces would not leave my mind.

When a friend asked me to share a trip to Southeast Asia this past winter, a trip that would include a week in Indonesia, it was the fulfillment of a dream. Of course I took my cameras.

We were not in Bali very long, but long enough to get some feeling of an enchanting harmony of man on his land, a harmony of life and art that we long for here in the West. But we

99

seem like the protagonist in *La Dolce Vita*, looking across the widening waters to an innocence that is forbidden to us.

Ever since I returned home from that trip, I have been haunted by the sound of water, the water of Bali—water that collects in the hollow craters of ancient volcanoes, water that rushes through canyons, ripples through deep riverbeds, trickles through the irrigation ditches, drop by drop, finally to reach the paddies mirroring the water-bearing clouds . . . water that bubbles up through the lava dust in a sacred spring . . . water that churns up from the lairs of ancient sea monsters—water of joy, water of plenty, water of terror—what monsters lurk beneath its sparkle? Which sail is the enemy's?—water wearing away the ancient stones, falling, seeking its level . . . everywhere water or its stylized counterpart. For the flash and spatter of notes from the Balinese gamelan, the marvelous orchestra of gongs, drums, and metallophones, have often been said to be those of that constant water that flows over and through and around the green island that Nehru called "the morning of the world."

Modern plane travel often follows ancient sea paths. Wind patterns and curiosity push traders and travelers in the same directions. We often appeared to be following the route of the Indian merchants who carried their religion of Hinduism, Buddhism, their art styles, their script, their laws, their myths and legends to the lands to the east and southeast that grew the precious spices they sought. Today the Hinduism and Buddhism brought from the northwest mingle with the animism and spirit worship of the islands to the east. Spirits—of the waterfall, the river, the sea, spirits of stones, of air and fire—lurk in the shadowy edges of life, make demands, challenge the powers of the ancestor gods to guide and protect.

Nature has powerful forces at her command. Harmony is the balance achieved among those forces. Evil is not conquered by pretending that it does not exist. Give it a place so that it will stay put and not attack. One learns to live in a kind of balance—with acts of ritual, prayers, and offerings appeasing the forces of evil. One of these offerings is dancing.

Dancers for the classical dances, such as the Legong, begin their training as small children, whose supple bodies older dancers massage, shape gently, urge into the patterns of the ancient and complex dance involving several characterizations and subtle interpretations of the changing moods of the music. Soon—as if the spirit of the older dancer had passed to the younger—the child moves off on her own, her own spirit and understanding now guiding her within the pattern. A fine dancer can truly be said to hold within himself the spirit of the god, his ancestor, as he makes his body, his art, an offering.

The temple is the heart of village life. In the dance performances that occur there the heroic legends of the *Ramayana* and *Mahabharata* show perfect beauty of spirit and body struggling against the forces of evil that would diminish the ancestor gods and betray their memory. The unseen ideal is ever-watching, inspiring the offering. Slender young bodies shaped to the weight of younger brothers and sisters curve easily into the positions of the dance. Small hands softened by massage bend into the backward crescent that art demands. Eyes turn inward in concentration and inner discipline. With exquisite harmony of movement and gesture the dancers strive for the perfection of the gods as portrayed in ancient sculptures.

The stones of Borobudur wear the stains of water like sheerest garments for the subtly carved bodies. Half obliterated by time, the ancestor gods of Prambanan perform their dances to the beat of the stone drums and metallophones.

Audiences, too, start young, as tiny infants sit in the laps of older children or grandparents, feeling the joys and terrors of the dramas they see, feeling the throb of the gamelan pulse through their bodies, unconsciously curving their fingers in imitation of the dancers'. They see very soon that the benevolent Barong will never really conquer Rangda the witch, for evil will always be part of life to struggle against; but there is always the perfect example of Rama, the incarnation of Vishnu, to guide one. And so they learn.

The gods, princes and princesses, fairies, benevolent monsters, magical birds and beasts—these become accessible to the farmer and to the small child alike. As the child grows, the stylization becomes lucid, the story clears.

An old Javanese treatise in Kawi, the ancient literary language of Java, states: "A man of condition should be versed in the history and literature of the past. He must know how to play the gamelan and understand the Kawi language. He must be clever in painting, wood carving, gold and iron work, needlework, the making of shadow puppets and musical instruments." Europe had no monopoly on Renaissance men!

Just as in the Italian *commedia dell'arte,* the cast of a Balinese play consists of stock characters: a king, his minister, a queen, her ladies, the witch, a monster, a rival, etc. To pass judgment on the exuberance of myths man has made to make comprehensible his universe may be as ludicrous as to judge eye color. Myths tell us who we are. They warn us of the monsters that lurk within us, as well as in the shadows of our world. They also point out the ideal of the hero whose mission it is to struggle and free us from our monsters. Giving body to his fears, the Balinese frees himself from them. His plays embrace the crudities and vulgarities of life simply because they, too, are always there.

It has been interesting to watch a little dog, docile and affectionate, in play revert to the ancestor wolf, stalk prey, shake it to break its back, suddenly stop and become once more the ingratiating pet. The flash of eye, the jagged tooth are always there beneath the surface.

The books we make with love and care and pass on to children often seem like pebbles cast into pools. The circles widen until the wavelets lap unseen shores. We in America have often been arrogant toward others as we watched them docilely handing over their rights. "Where were the honest?" "Where were the good?" We didn't see quite how it could happen to us. The glitter of sun fire on the waters bedazzles us until we see the jagged fin and the flash of fangs—and decide to uncover our own.

In the fifties many painters discovered what dancers, musicians, potters—also masons and housepainters—have known for a long time—that the act of doing something could be such an intense experience that that act became an end in itself, more important that the result. The means became the message. The fun and sheer brashness of pop art pushed many of us to take a fresh look at our supermarket culture, and then minimal art, and the term *art* became so diffuse that it has lost most of its meaning, as less is more, until nothing may be everything, and sometimes the opposite also true.

Like water, all these movements seep down through layers of commercial art and leave their stains on children's books. And if the books have any life, they leave their stains on the children.

Clichés so often seem only that until one has lived through them oneself. Photography versus drawing? Where is the versus? Books versus filmstrips, or dance, or paintings, or theatre? Go deep enough and won't our points converge? In styles as various as the people who create them, the new and old tales get told—that the peacocking tiger will become a mouse, the fisherman's wife's palace will become a hovel, the betinseled little fir tree, always yearning for more, will end up on the rubbish heap.

The child who has been given his heritage goes armed to meet his monsters on that distant shore. There will be contests, disillusion, and fresh starts. But he will not be entirely alone. Our fresh streams stink with wastes; we send our brooks through cement culverts so they won't be in our way. But the springs from the deep earth still bubble up and find their path and slowly wear their grooves in the rock until the pool mirrors the wide sky.

ONE WONDERS

"Wells don't fill without showers."

One wonders if twenty or thirty years from now this middle of the century period of children's book illustration will not seem a spectacular flowering.

The last ten years have seen a dramatic expansion in the publishing of books for children. There have been more children than ever before. In order to reap some of the rewards of this market, many publishers formerly not particularly interested in children's books have hastened to form or enlarge juvenile departments. In the consolidated houses made from mergers of two or more companies, several juvenile departments may function under the direction of one managing editor. Much actual editing of manuscripts had to be relegated to associates and assistants. The entry of the communications industry into publishing mergers is bound to have a future effect on publishing in general, and on publishing books for children. The output of books shows almost everywhere the effects of this expansion, and the children and the adolescents and adults they will become will be bound to feel and show it too.

Published in *Illustrators of Children's Books: 1957–1966* by *The Horn Book*, Boston 1968.

Warehouse storage costs are high, often higher than reprinting costs. Because book ordering is now and will become more and more centralized, teachers, librarians, and parents depend on selected lists, on reviews, on the selection of prize books and their runners-up to guide them in their ordering.

Awards proliferate, and while they act as a stimulus for improving quality, they also have a very great commercial importance. A few books attain a prominence that may be disproportionate to their aesthetic importance and to their value to children. Understandably eager for the publicity and long life assured a prize book, publishers sometimes produce books that appear to be designed to catch the eye of awarding committees, fortunately not always bedazzled by such blandishments. The fact that often on such committees are some people who use books with children probably means that many choices, if not distinguished, might be books that speak to children. One will always wonder about awards—and the wonderment is probably a good thing. It would be sad if there were not conflicting opinions about outstanding books. That there are so many deserving strong support is a sign of health.

To look over the bulk of picture books and illustrated books for young children published in the past ten years is a stimulating, often exhilarating, chastening, saddening, and eventually numbing experience. Stimulating because there is a tremendous variety of vital and very skillful work being done—and because sure, fresh talents like Margot Zemach, Leo Lionni, Janina Domanska, Beni Montresor, Celestino Piatti, Marvin Bileck, Bernarda Bryson, Joseph Low, Tomi Ungerer, Anita Lobel, Edward Sorel, Nicolas Sidjakov, Ann Grifalconi, Nonny Hogrogian, and many others from a variety of countries and backgrounds have brought individuality and fresh points of view to the field. Many illustrators active earlier have constantly renewed themselves and grown. Chastening because among the huge numbers of books published there is slight chance for the individual book to reach children already bombarded with visual stimuli. Saddening because despite the brilliant highlights, the general picture adds up to grayness. Numbing because brighter and brighter, smarter and smarter, they come pouring off the presses. The streams that supply this torrent are hardly deep enough to quench the tremendous thirst for talent.

Attracted perhaps by the financial rewards in a thriving industry but more probably by a realization that in illustration for children an artist can work honestly, freely, and imaginatively, many artists from other fields of artwork have been drawn to children's books. Once past the adults who are barriers or bridges between the book and the child, these artists can draw their personal brand of poetry or nonsense or magic and hope that someone will see it and look at it and understand it. They are fairly sure of having an appreciative audience. But an illustrator for young children would do well to look over that barrier or bridge and consider the child beyond.

Stage design, poster-making, advertising, printmaking, painting—all kinds of artwork have given a special flavor and reference to the work of artists in picture books. An artist draws on his own experience, his family, his travels, his life other than that connected with books. He needs variety as much as he needs concentration. Between books, many artists return to painting, to printmaking, to entirely different pursuits. Wells don't fill without showers. When one can predict the look of a book, when one knows the subject and the name of the artist and can be reasonably accurate in one's predictions, one can wonder how such an artist looks at his own growth and his obligation to develop himself. The artists who remain freshest and bring a sense of a new experience to what they do seem to be those whose work flows back and forth between books and other activities.

The corps of illustrators for young children in this country is never static. The field is constantly in flux. Some names have dropped out; many others have been added. Some who have made a brilliant contribution, such as Nicolas Mordvinoff, have returned to their own painting or sculpture. Children will miss seeing new, engagingly childlike pictures by Françoise, more dashing cocks and cats of Hans Fischer, or powerfully simple paintings of A. Birnbaum. All these artists are irreplaceable, for they spoke in very individual styles.

Some illustrators seem to have an inexhaustible capacity to renew themselves and maintain through many books a look of freshness. Whether changing direction or style from time to time or continually deepening and intensifying one they had already followed, their work has been of a consistently high level.

Working in black-and-white line or tinted drawings, Erik Blegvad carries on a tradition we have associated with Ernest Shepard. His decorations and illustrations on a small scale are very accessible to a child and provide the comfort of the known without ever sinking into the mannered or the banal. Edward Ardizzone has demonstrated in many illustrated books and picture books his flair for storytelling, emphasizing now atmosphere, now the heroics a child feels about his own acts. With just enough line to define his characters and hatched tone in a variety of values, he creates a whole atmospheric world. Whether picturing children or animals, Symeon Shimin, by his intensity and dedication, lifts extreme realism to a level of great beauty. William Pène Du Bois creates his own private brand of fantasy, finicky and fascinating. Leonard Everett Fisher and Anthony Ravielli have lifted technical scientific drawing to a level of beauty as well as accuracy. With delicacy and great charm Adrienne Adams has pictured children's observations of nature and has reillustrated beloved folk and fairy tales. Evaline Ness's beautiful drawings for *Sam, Bangs & Moonshine* suggest the bleakness of a northern fishing port. The characterizations of Sam and her friend Thomas are delightful. A master of design of space and pattern, she has reached with this book a new depth of feeling.

Perhaps more than any other illustrator, Roger Duvoisin has maintained a fresh point of view in his picture books. Children all over the world have followed the adventures of his beloved Happy Lion, Petunia the goose, or Veronica the hippopotamus. With wit and affection he draws characters that are true in feeling to both the animals they are and the people they resemble.

Artists from other countries, whether living here or abroad, continue to enlarge our own way of feeling. To our children and to our own artists they often bring a tradition of good graphic design, memories, and visions from two worlds. The exchange is always richer, as publishers here and abroad add to their own lists by reprinting books from other countries. Some of our handsomest picture books have first been published abroad, printed to standards we can scarcely meet in this country. Many styles of working have become international as a result of these exchanges.

Fortunately, many styles exist side by side, some exquisitely finished hangovers or harkbacks to an earlier period of luxury editions; some vigorous reflections of the immediate present, some prognostications of a future climate in children's books, produced more hastily and more carelessly as publishers try to beat labor and production costs.

One doesn't really have to wonder why more publishers have turned to other countries with strong traditions in printing—Holland, Switzerland, Italy, Germany, and now, Japan—

for the excellence they require. Printing costs may be lower abroad, but skill is refined and abundant. There is a popular saying that American printers can give better results if they want to—if they could afford the time. After leafing through hundreds of garish and poorly printed books, with muddy color work, blurred registry, pale and blurred type, one wonders. . . . The inferiority of the printing in many of these books is ironic, because the publisher has quite obviously offered the artist freedom to use a variety of graphic processes, of painting techniques.

The old battles of twenty years ago, in which partisans for the new and for open-mindedness championed the right of contemporary and even far-out types of illustration to find their way to children, have been won. To see how completely, one has only to look at artwork of children themselves, taught in modes derived from the most sophisticated of contemporary art.

Painters have occasionally turned to illustration for children, with varying success. Ben Shahn's drawings for *Ounce Dice Trice* by Alastair Reid are as freshly conceived as the collection of out-of-the-ordinary words and nonsense that make up the text. The line spins and sings, snares the objects in its loops, whizzing around the book with the quick pleasure one feels in the words. Such books are perhaps not for every child but a very special delight for some children.

Artists with a strong feeling for the possibilities of flat color, like Roger Duvoisin and Nicolas Mordvinoff, have constantly experimented to further their limited means and have come up with results that rival fine prints in graphic interest. They manipulate—scratch, rub, stipple, and blot—their plastic separation plates; but their line color remains part of a planographic printing scheme that goes with type. Over-printing of the colors extends the number of colors but gives an overall harmony difficult to achieve with process colors. The artist relies on his own inventiveness to get the most out of little and make little speak more powerfully. At its best, hand-separated flat color has a beauty that suggests that of a stone lithograph.

Laymen show an increasing and often touching interest in the techniques of illustration and bookmaking. A few short workshop sessions can aid one in understanding that illustrators and publishers do have problems. But one wonders at the attempt to absorb in so short a time knowledge of skills acquired over many years by artists constantly experimenting. It is as if "how," once known, will answer "why?" No age is too old for learning to look, but one wonders if a more thoughtful attention to "why?" on the part of laymen might not be more useful to children and their books. One wonders when library schools and colleges of education will add more courses in aesthetics to their curricula and start young teachers and librarians on a course of more perceptive examination of what they are called upon to judge and distribute.

One wonders if the interest in techniques has resulted in better aesthetic judgment. One wonders how much it helps to know if a picture was done in crayon or wash, woodcut or acrylic, if one does not see that the artist woefully missed the point and mood of the story he was illustrating; if hands that are meant to hold, can't; if images crowd the page and distort the focus and meaning of the story and suffocate its message. Much of the attention accorded some types of illustration seems to depend on the isolated picture, often very beautiful and fascinating as an object, with almost no regard for whether or not it serves the text well. Judges of illustration can hardly have time to read all the books they are called upon to examine. Their decisions can be enlightening but are most valuable if laymen follow them up by reading and looking at the books and wondering.

113

Graphic styles change, of course. It is hard to tell as one looks over the books of the last ten years whether much of the bookmaking one sees is a preview of change in the form of the book as we have known it or is the result of haste in planning or ineptitude on the part of artists and editors in the niceties of bookmaking.

Is it poor planning or greed for space in the average thirty-two-page book that crowds title page and ever-burgeoning copyright information forward right onto the endpapers? The child opens the book as if he turns on a shower faucet. Bang! He's in it. It is hard to tell whether a child is conscious of the beauty or suitability of a title page or if he feels the serenity of enough front matter to ease him into the expectation of pleasure.

With understandable pride publishers seize on any recognition that singles out their books from the crowd. But one wonders about the taste for placing publicity write-ups stressing awards, really hard-sell advertising, in the body of the book instead of on the jacket flap.

Book printing is a small part of the business of offset-printing plants, which get larger and more lucrative contracts from the publishers of glossy magazines and advertising. Picture books have to be fitted into tight printing schedules. More and more attention is being given to cutting time costs. Photographic typesetting can eliminate the casting of the lead slug and provide film for stripping in on the negatives for making the offset plates. Some books have been set with IBM typewriters. One wonders if there will not be a technical changeover in typesetting similar to the change from letterpress to offset about twenty-five years ago.

A book budget may not permit the fine work the reproduction of illustration needs—the color-proving of the whole book before the final run and the proper hand-cleaning of negatives. Color-mixing is often done to formula in a job lot by the ink manufacturer, and a press is fortunate to have one man who really knows how to mix color and can direct the subtle adjustments that make the difference between banality or beauty in color printing.

With the technical advances made in offset lithography, it does not cost very much more to print a four-color book than it does a two- or three-. After the ink colors are set and approved on the huge four-color presses, the press time is much the same. The cost of additional negatives is less than that of the running time of the presses. From looking at the books, one wonders if some have thought that since a book will cost very little more to print in four colors, why print it in fewer? Why not give it all the color possible? Artists, slightly drunk with the freedom they thought they needed for the full expression of their ideas, have gone overboard with color. Intrigued with all the expressive possibilities of their material, they have explored and exploited every nuance of the story. In a desire to add something of their own to a text, they sometimes have created a counterpoint of design, textures, and details that overwhelm the main theme. One wonders . . . do they find their themes too square? Do they mistrust their simplicity, their obviousness? Or do they just not understand them and their needs?

The time is probably coming when fewer artists will be asked to do color separations. We are seeing more reproductions of elaborate painting techniques as illustration in children's books. Some of these, meticulously finished, hark back to the deluxe and lush editions of an earlier period that were hardly published for the average child.

New standards in bookmaking and new graphic standards will undoubtedly arise as those we traditionally associate with the book breakdown. The exhibitions of children's books

115

selected by the American Institute of Graphic Arts have stim-
ulated an interest in book design and bookmaking. The judges
have deplored the banal bindings of trade editions, side sew-
ing that sucks in pictures and prevents a book from being held
open easily; the mediocrity of illustration in many older children's books; and a general carelessness in manufacturing.
Some of their catalogues list all details of production and let
the books and their selection speak for themselves. Others
admit to a coy confusion of standards among the judges, dis-
paraging their own choices or praising them out of all proportion to their achievement. But the recognition of the need for
good design in a young child's book plus the publicity that
recognition is now receiving are having an effect in raising
their quality.

Certain trends, probably developing long before 1956 but
much more noticeable now because there are more books,
stand out as one looks back over the ten years. One sees
fewer books with illustrations inspired by animated cartoons,
and, in general, books have a smarter, more "sophisticated"
look in color and design. The banal, pastel children of an earlier period have grown up and given way to a new lot of self-
conscious little creatures, with chevron mouths up or down,
and chevron eyes. Sometimes they are amusing in a wry and
satirical way. One wonders what children see in them. Do
they see themselves so? One can hardly believe in their
gaiety. They look out at us, ever alert to see if we don't find
them charming.

The experimentation in the last ten years has moved away
from the pop-ups, the "feelies" and obvious tricks to attract
attention, and is more concerned with ideas. A whole group
of books is designed to enter the world of the child as it were
at his height. Sometimes they speak to him in his own words;
sometimes they lead him out of and beyond his immediate

world. Probably because there were very gifted designers to do them, a group of designers' books has appeared. At their best, without quite the order of poetry, these books are beautiful, or instructive, or playful, or provocative, and often all four. While not attempting illustration as we have usually thought of it, these artists have used objects and design elements with great freshness. Occasionally it is impossible to find in them any clear demarcation between design and illustration.

Bringing to his books experience in children's theatre and a very sure understanding of children's senses of humor, Remy Charlip has designed some very original and amusing books: with Burton Supree, *Mother Mother I feel Sick, Send for the Doctor, Quick, Quick, Quick; Dress Up; Fortunately*. In them he uses the simplest of visual elements. With his stylized drawings for *Four Fur Feet*, however, he moves into very subtle illustration of the poetic text as the child turns the book to the curve of the mysterious beast's walk around the world.

When a designer-illustrator oversees every detail of the physical book, the results can be very beautiful. Taking her cue from old Armenian manuscripts, Nonny Hogrogian has designed and made simple but vivid drawings for *Once There Was and Was Not*, a collection of Armenian tales by Virginia Tashjian.

Ellen Raskin has brought a beautiful sense of design to her books illustrated with woodcuts, Dylan Thomas's *A Child's Christmas in Wales*, Ruth Krauss's *Mama, I Wish I was Snow: Child, You'd Be Very Cold*, and Blake's *Songs of Innocence*.

William Wondriska has linked styles and sizes to objects and the objects that make them.

Ivan Chermayeff's deceptively simple flat-color illustrations for *The Thinking Book* are immediately accessible to a child. In their naïve spirit they suggest a child's drawings without copying them. His amusing pictures for Ogden Nash's *The New Nutcracker Suite and Other Innocent Verses* escape the banality of much of the pictured humor that is rather sophisticated for children.

Paul Rand's vivid posterlike images are essences born of enormous skill in distilling a visual point to its most telling simplicity. Although a bit subtle for an average child of picture-book age, his designs developed around the words by Ann Rand are stimulaing in idea. *Little 1* is a kind of tour de force in giving personality to the number 1.

There is a constant effort to say old things in new ways to children. One sometimes wonders if the urge to experiment is not a stronger drive than concern with the substance of a book. Picture-book format is obvious for books that are primarily visual. There are some artist-designers who have moved very confidently from the world of adult design to that of children, for perhaps the best of both worlds is interchangeable. But one wonders about the reaction of a little child who picks up some of the books that are clever experiments in typography, in color design, in attempts to enter his private world of imaginative play.

Production costs for some time deterred the publishing of an American edition of Bruno Munari's *nella notte buia*, recently issued by Wittenborn, a publisher of art books. Here very simple elements do not function in the normal continuity of illustrations for a story but serve a poetic idea of some depth. The child is led gently to see and feel that there is more to what he looks at than what he notices at first. At the same time the artist retains the simplicity of his first vision of a natural phenomenon. Caves can tell of the history of the earth, or of man, but a little light in the sky need not be a star to be a delight to the eye.

Artists and editors could well study Munari's picture books.

Simple, handsome without being self-conscious, these pictures are informed by a sense of play akin to the child's own, yet respecting his. They are directed by warmth. They prove the absurdity of dogma about what one does for children. They start from a core of affection, with respect for the child's mind and for his own strengths and an awareness of his sense of play, yet are equally aware that the adult who tries to do likewise can fall into the false coyness that exploits that very same playfulness in some of our books.

In recent years we have seen many more books using prints as illustrations. Woodcut is a medium that demands from artists a special fondness for its particular qualities and its harmony with type. The texture of wood, the very force needed to cut it, its tendency to splinter and ruin a line make it a tough vehicle for visual ideas small enough for a book page. But the richness of wood grain, the vigor of a cut line, the variety of tonal effects possible with different kinds of cutting and gouging, the brilliant contrasts between whites and darks, the beautiful colors possible with overprinting one color on another — all these make it a very attractive medium for some types of illustration. Many printmakers have been using it in children's books.

Woodcut is not a medium to be applied to any kind of subject, but occasionally no other would be quite so effective in telling a particular story. Illustrators sometimes misuse it or do not exploit the very qualities that make it unique when they force it to say what pen-and-ink or painted flat colors can say. Woodcut prints photographed and printed in halftone lose the graphic harmony between cut line and type and disrupt the optical unity of a page. The mixture of woodcut with other media—with collage, with crayon and pen line — sometimes appears to be a makeshift solution to a problem, though it need not be. Inventiveness sometimes outstrips imagination.

One wonders, when one sees an almost identical piece of wood texture serving in book after book as sunrise, sunset, water, clouds—with other printed or drawn images superimposed—was the artist hard up to find another piece of wood?

To Antonio Frasconi woodcut is just as much a natural language as Italian or Spanish or English. It serves him for whatever he has to say. There is no barrier between the artist and the viewer. His woodcuts are internationally known. His books for children, often somber in mood, thoughtful, but always handsome and very expressive, reflect his own belief that a child should be helped to move out of himself toward an understanding and perception of the world. Here is artistic responsibility of great depth put at the service of childhood. A feeling artist can put texture and found wood shapes into a poetic context that extends the image it serves and so stimulate an awareness of the unity underlying the similar forces in differing materials.

John and Clare Ross have interpreted the sweep of Whitman, the staccato patterns of city life, in woodcuts for older children. Philip Reed has designed exquisite volumes illustrated with charming wood engravings in color. Leonard Everett Fisher has raised scratchboard technique to the level of fine wood engraving. Blair Lent has used his prints most imaginatively in *The Wave,* filling space with shapes—the gray rolls of thunder, the billowing wave, the tumbling jumble of houses, temples, and boats. Here stylization of the forms is a powerful element in their expressiveness. Joseph Low has moved from stylization to an engaging and unhackneyed spontaneity in his drawings and linoleum cuts. The washes of thin color under his prints, a technique commonly used in advertising and in illustrations, always seem fresh and not arbitrary.

Collage has long been known to children's books and has a

lively background in cut-paper work. But collage as a medium for illustration, making full use of its capacity for visual metaphor, has flowered in the last ten years.

The urge to invent can easily defeat itself. When the pattern and variety of textures speak too insistently and call attention to themselves as objects instead of subordinating themselves to the picture, collage can be confusing and spotty or overloaded. A child sees a collection of textures more or less resembling the images he looks for. Without some kind of underlying emotional organization and warmth, the artist may have given him strong design, but lace, fabrics, and feathers instead of a dignified old man; bits of existence, but not a living creature. A sea can remain chaotic blocks of blue and green paper.

In his two picture books about a little boy enjoying a snowy day or learning to whistle, Ezra Jack Keats has used collage very charmingly, using French marbled papers, wallpaper, Japanese silk papers—a great variety of textures and colors as background to his simple and childlike stories. The shape of the brown child making an accent against the white or light backgrounds is beautiful. All the visual elements work together to tell the story.

Leo Lionni is one of the most imaginative artists of collage, so skillful that one thinks first of the picture and only later of the means he used. In his *Inch by Inch* there is a scaffold of very lively drawing. The motif of the blades of grass recurs as the inchworm moves along through the book. Each component texture extends the expressiveness of the drawing; the artist confines himself to only those textures and colors needed to carry the inchworm along. In *Swimmy* he stamps, blots, superimposes prints of lace on his blotted watercolor washes. The blotted wet pictures suggest the beautiful, vague, and mysterious world under the sea, where menace and fear are precise if the definitions of that world are not. The technique here always serves the idea.

Simplicity is not always strength, nor does an apparently naïve technique reveal simplicity of spirit. At its best, simplicity is a matured richness distilled to its essence, the end of the progress of a creative idea, not the beginning.

With circles and strips of torn paper, the simplest possible means, Lionni made *little blue and little yellow*. It is a profound little book, gay enough to make a child laugh aloud but wise about color mixtures, about judging by appearances, about recognizing the changes brought about by friendship and love. Lionni uses collage with poetic economy.

Little children are reputed to like brilliant colors. Because many easel artists have vivid imaginations and there is money to earn in the lucrative picture-book field, some painters who are accustomed to work very freely have turned to the picture book. Occasionally one feels they have become so engrossed in their own picture-making they have forgotten that child on the other side of the bridge and are doing pictures for the bridge itself. A public that buys garish commodities stimulates the publishers to put out more of the same and other artists to go and do likewise. One suspects that some painters enter children's book illustration by mistake. Their misunderstanding of the scale of artwork to a book page, their use of heavy painting techniques with thick impasto that overwhelm a simple narrative lead one to wish they had learned more about what a picture book is. One wonders if some artists don't have their editors hypnotized. The axe that should fall on an overwritten text and overcolored, overblown pictures remains suspended, and the overripe offering is sent out.

A host of extremely competent and often gifted illustrators have turned from advertising to children's books. They bring brilliantly stylized techniques, often in a hatched pen line, a professional finish to their overall design, and a lively experimentation with shape and format. Many show an endless care in fashioning, in shaping flaccid images into solidity. Styles of draughtsmanship make their own laws, but if one subscribes to traditional conventions in perspective, in the movements possible to human joints, in the space three-dimensional objects occupy, then one must follow through. All the finish in the world cannot disguise the inadequacies of some illustration, the banal color, the failure to respect the facts of the text.

Each period sprouts its own fashions. Clichés multiply when more and more people work hastily and there is little time to digest experience or impressions before giving them forth again. One copies what one has done or what one has seen, often unconsciously.

One can never know whether a child of today, accustomed to supermarket shelves, is startled to find the same repetition of objects lined up in his books. Soldiers, processions—some subjects lend themselves to lineups; some are submerged in repetitive hammering. What starts imaginatively with one image can multiply into a numerical insistence that is as dull and impersonal as those supermarket shelves.

Felix Hoffmann, who has drawn distinguished and beautiful new editions of Grimm, has made of the old verse *A Boy Went Out to Gather Pears* a sturdy and methodical but beautiful little book. Each repetition of the woodcut elements adds something new to the story.

Because in this period many classics published near the turn of the century have passed into public domain, publishers have rushed to reissue them, often in competition with the orginal, and in editions carelessly or lovingly photographed from the old editions. The arguments about definitive editions go on, not really solving anything, because all that is lacking is the appearance of an artist so capable of entering freshly into the spirit of a book that earlier, loved editions move over to make room for his.

In a recent trade publication a well-known critic wondered out loud about some recent editions of classics. She placed a photograph of a picture from a recent edition publicized as "definitive" next to one from the famous British artist who so clearly had been the more-than-inspiration. In comparing the two, one noticed that on page after page of the new edition only a background would be added to a vulgarized redrawing of the original. Could such similarities in characterization and composition be accidents? Responsible parents and librarians can deplore such practices, but they can only discourage the publication of such ersatz editions by examination, comparison, and choice of the genuine.

It doesn't even take a glance down our glass-and-steel city streets to see why we are in many ways turning back to a cozier age in some of our illustration. There has been a great spurt of what one could call neo-Victorianism—a harking back to styles of drawing based on the pen-and-ink techniques, the steel and wood engravings of the last century, and a world apparently fuller of a number of things than ours is. One of the most successful using these techniques, always at the service of his own wit and feeling, is Maurice Sendak. In his illustrations for the tales of Wilhelm Hauff and Frank Stockton, In the exquisite books of Randall Jarrell, he recreates a silvery world, meticulously delineated, in which a child can walk around; but at the same time he is keeping alive one of the most vital traditions in children's book illustration—that of Richard Doyle, Tenniel, and Cruikshank. Plagiarism is an ugly word and an uglier practice. While they are strengthening their own illustration and finding their own ways, young artists understandably imitate the styles they admire and that they relate to temperamentally. A successful and popular artist like Sendak has hosts of imitators of the square little children in some of his picture books. Without the personal motivation of the orginals, they remain imitations.

One wonders if young artists are sometimes urged to try someone else's style. As in the old tale of the mixed-up feet, is it too difficult for them to find their own when asleep? Watch and wait is all we can do.

With expressive distortions, elongations, compressions, an artist's line follows the impulses of his nerves and feeling, the meanderings of his imagination. The character of a book shows up in the character of the lines in its illustrations—wispy and delicate in the watercolor drawings of Alois Carigiet; blunt and monolithically emphatic in the poster images of Celestino Piatti; crystalline in the crowded details of Marvin Bileck; elegantly simple in the clean lines of Reiner Zimnik. Style in illustration as in writing has a good deal to say about an artist's involvement with his material, his focus, his aims. Why did he do this particular book? Sometimes how he did it can tell us something about why.

Who presumes to reillustrate the verses of Edward Lear is up against formidable competition from Mr. Lear himself. Lear has never really been out of fashion with children. Several artists have recently challenged his drawings with their own or have tried to draw humor in a similar vein.

Tomi Ungerer has the keenest sense of the absurd. Beneath an air of innocent gaiety is a very acute wit. His drawings for *Oh, What Nonsense!* a collection of humorous poems edited by William Cole, are delightful in the directness of their line.

With gentle satire and great delicacy Barbara Cooney has recreated the woeful little tragedy of Cock Robin. The satire never bursts out of the miniature frame of the story. In an unassuming but very skillful way she has been extremely successful in her illustrations for Lear. Her drawings seem extensions of his, so completely has she caught their quality.

Perhaps because of the recognition granted some illustrated fairy tales, but more probably because of the response of children to them in libraries, there has been an enormous number of new editions of old favorites and, once the better known ones were between covers, of those not so well known. Tales, humorous and fanciful, fables, tall tales, hero legends, myths—there is hardly a type of narrative that has not appeared with illustrations. The challenge to an illustrator of such stories is much greater than that of the books mentioned earlier. A line of intensity must not only be maintained but must build as the story does; characters must be vivid, must occasionally develop inwardly as well as outwardly; compositions of pages must constantly change although dealing with the same basic background. Each element contributes to the power of the telling and helps determine the atmosphere of the story.

Humorous, robust tales have been particularly successful as individual books. One of the stongest new talents to emerge in the last ten years is Margot Zemach. Compare *The Three Sillies, Nail Soup, The Speckled Hen* with any of several treatments of folktales with the same earthy origins and feel the sureness of her comic vision, the core of warmth in the observation of human foibles and absurdities. The constant invention always remains within the textual framework of the story—witness the stranger in the inn with head down, changing his trousers. Her large-nosed, black-stockinged women look surprised at being caught in ridiculous situations. Here is a very sure touch; the absurd is met head on. This artist gives every promise of growing as she extends the emotional range of her material.

Andersen is one of the most demanding of authors for an

illustrator. While some illustrators picture the facts of his stories delightfully, the deeper meanings elude them, glossed over in favor of a pretty charm. The child gets no hint that here is something more than a barnyard fable or an average fairy tale. It is easy to be beguiled by the trappings of a period, to become enmeshed in researches and lose the poetic significance of these distillates from several folk origins through the mind and heart of a most unusual man. But what a child remembers is more apt to be the poetic truth of the story than the factual truth of the pictures, if the artist has approached his task with understanding of that truth. Probably not for every illustrator, the stories of Andersen present rare challenges and rare satisfactions for one who is willing to submit himself to them.

Children have been handed all kinds of translations and all kinds of illustrations of Andersen, from the deluxe, to the sweet, to the cozy. Adrienne Adams, Maurice Sendak, Erik Blegvad, Bill Sokol, and Nancy Burkert are some of the artists who have reinterpreted Andersen.

Editors only occasionally have had an active background in sharing books with children in storytelling. Librarians who have that background would do well to think of the values they subscribe to and their responsibility to the children and to the poet whose words may live in them. If one is courageous enough to tell some of these stories to children, desperate, terror-stricken stories shot with beauty and illuminated by courage and sacrifice, one should choose illustrated versions that face the issues of the stories. To judge from some of the recent editions of folk and fairy tales, one wonders at the emotional and spiritual involvement of the artists who did them. Their books are often brilliant but shallow. They have rushed in where humility, wit, and vitality of imagination might have guided them.

Many illustrators have tried to write—with varying success—and occasionally authors have tried to draw—with less. One feels that the desire to do a book may be commendable; but without something to say to children and the means to say it, or even the desire to develop the means, one wonders at the arrogance that expects a child to be interested in half-baked creations, texts or pictures. There is still among laymen a lack of comprehension of the discipline needed to pare a text to a basic line that looks simple. A picture book is as concise as poetry. Text and pictures combine to form an essence that expands in the child's mind.

One wonders why some artists, masters of subjective, poetic stylizations, turn to picture books. Do their editors urge them, or aren't they able to stop them? Their characters are forced into uncomfortable stylizations that strain away most of their feelings.

In the drive to produce more books there is a tendency to take one poem and make a book of it. This is particularly successful with narrative poems and ballads. One wonders whether with the increasing picturing of fantasy, the illustration of subjective poetry will be eventually stultifying or stimulating to the imagination of a child.

As we look ahead to a future of greater technical advances, more urbanization and more centralized control of all our communications, one wonders. . . . The enormous power to create opinion and a whole climate of taste will mean enormous responsibilities. The possibility of a kind of brainwashing and control of attitudes of children through their books will have to be faced by all those working for children.

Already not to be *with* it is to many not to be at all. The nervous, jittery activity of very competitive city life will have its effect on children. That more young children will have access to books could mean more dedicated and brilliant invention by our artists.

The heritage of the folktale is one of the most vital possessions we can pass on to children. The renaissance of the folktale as an individual book for young children is perhaps one of the most valuable trends in the past ten years. The chance for the appearance of many brilliant, original books is always slim. But one wonders if the base of simple, earthy wisdom and the observation of humanity going about its living, trying to scale the mountains of its visions—the chance for the odd one who is usually *not* with it to succeed—may not be our most important gifts to children from this period.

IN AND OUT OF TIME

*"Tell it, chant it, dance it, play it,
paint it—life is infinitely precious."*

Each year, about now, in Connecticut, the gray lines of winter blur into green, the stream rushes white, and the marsh vibrates with the cry of the peeper. And our house vibrates with the cries of flutes, and struggles. I play the flute, not very well, but well enough to give me some idea of the music that has always been a part of my life. Say "flute"and some eyes shine and mouths whisper in awe, "Rampal!" Others hear Pan out in the hemlocks. But no matter how lyrical you wax, you are the despair of anyone who wants to play with you if you can't beat time. And the crucial little word is "and." The counting is only up to six, with those little "and's" clarifying everything—almost.

Since I didn't learn this as a child and I am determined to play better, I am very much aware of time these days. I try to hear once more the words of dear teachers of twenty years ago, not really feeling like offering my struggles to any present one. The old words ring true.

Regina Medal Acceptance speech given at the annual conference of the Catholic Library Association, San Francisco, Calif., 1977. Published in *Catholic Library World,* July–August 1977.

When I write, I hear a brilliant, also patient, teacher, trying to cope with my lush rhapsodies: "Just write me *one* clear sentence!" When I paint and draw, I see the radiant face of a beloved painter, gasping with emphysema: "But each morning I can feel I'm alive, can't I?" And his words live on after him. And the brief mutters of another painter, with perhaps the clearest mind I have ever known personally: "Think what color will make *this* space work." Another teacher, of Greek literature: "But you can't think in a vacuum!"

These strands that go back in time are now like those aerial threads by which each year's batch of young spiders migrates to a new home to avoid the cannibalism of their brothers. But long ago they were reins, guidelines. For some of us time gets turned around. We are young when all our senses tell us we are old. Many years ago, a young librarian at a conference like this saw me for the first time and was so astonished her tongue outran her head, and she blurted out, "Your books are young, but you are old!" Probably better that than the other way around.

None of us popped full-blown out from under Jove's eyebrow. For each of us there was probably someone back there urging, showing, pointing out, even giving us the smack that sent us off on our road. The wisest teachers teach for all time, any time, and we hear their words freshly applicable all our lives.

In her haunting and powerful little book, *Tuck Everlasting,* Natalie Babbitt writes of the tragedy of a family that has stumbled on the secret of everlasting life, has fallen off time's wheel, and is cursed to stay as it is, homeless in a world of change.

"It's a wheel, Winnie. Everything's a wheel, turning and turning, never stopping. The frogs is part of it, and the bugs, and the fish, and the wood thrush, too. And people. But never the same ones. Always coming in new, always growing and changing, and always moving on. That's the way it's supposed to be. That's the way it *is*."

Perhaps how we *do* for children depends on how we *see* them in time. From the inside, time for them seems endless: "How long until . . . " and "I can't wait for. . . ." But from the outside, we turn our backs on them for a few minutes and they've shot up several inches; and picture books are given to biologists and lawyers by doting aunts. Sometimes we treat these great abrupt children like mass and push them into precocity that spreads them thin in parts of their lives that might have enriched them later on. Within that child stretching so tall is the sponge-mind of the future adult and the heart that, like any muscle, needs exercise for health.

When I saw the list of former recipients of the Regina Medal, it was as if a merry-go-round had done a backward turn. So many names there had been directly or indirectly part of my life, and some were friends—unflappable, calm people pursuing excellence, probably praying to themselves, "May I be adequate—to nail down what is in my head, to stand loyal to my own values." Their steadiness was like a calm deep, far below the wind-ruffled surface of everyday.

Nietzche wrote that "there should ever and again be men among you able to elevate you to *your* heights: that is the prize for which you strive." *Our Crowd, A Goodly Heritage, The Brave Company, We Happy Few, Let's Get Well, A Night of Watching:* few such titles are preposterous applied to such a company, for their names call up memories of fellowship, of joy in sharing an intensity of inner direction in service to the developing spirit of children.

There they were: Eleanor Farjeon, writing encouraging letters to a friend directing *The Glass Slipper,* for which I did costumes and settings for her child players. Anne Carroll Moore, in a red dress, deep voice reading nonsense with the wit of wisdom. How, from that then frail body, so much reasonance and strength? Great guide, with a ready ear for the ideas of young people, mythmaker, celebrant of spirit, and finally, dear, warm friend. There was Fred Melcher in a red cloak, white beard and miter, launching the Christmas celebration in the Central Children's Room of the New York Public Library on St. Nicholas Eve; showing the *kama shibai* he had brought back from a State Department mission to Japan. His pockets yielded the delightful little early children's books he treasured; his warmth filled the room, as did his desire to recognize distinction as it happened in books. Frances Clarke Sayers, whose meetings were celebrations of the joy of sharing the products of mind and spirit, and who charmed writers like Lewis Mumford, Carl Sandburg, Jean Charlot to share their thoughts with those who went back refreshed to share theirs with children. There are the storytellers: Padraic Colum and Ruth Sawyer Durand, sharing with such relish from their bags of tales. *The Voyage of the Wee Red Cap* is now forever part of Christmas in my mind.

Publishers, librarians, storytellers, some, like Anne Carroll Moore and Virginia Haviland, world citizens in their more than national concern for children's books. And there are the bookmakers: Lynd Ward, whose *Ching-Li and the Dragons* and *The Cat Who Went to Heaven* for children and *God's Angry Man* for adults, gave me an idea of the passion and lyricism that one could put into illustration, opened my eyes to what a picture book could be, extending way beyond the book in the hand. Marguerite de Angeli, one of the first illustrators I was aware of. I saw some of her early, unmistakably individual work in our Sunday school papers, long before I knew *Henner's Lydia*. How the picture books of Robert McCloskey— *Lentil, Make Way for Ducklings*—the condensed accuracy of real humor based on life—livened my picture-book hours. The care of the d'Aulaires, spent on those ever-fresh evocations of Norwegian childhood in stone lithography, one of the most lovely of mediums for illustration. Bertha Mahoney Miller, telling of love's labor in the bookshop that grew into *The Horn Book.*

There are many others, whose medal gold was the love and esteem of those with whom and for whom they served, the letters finding their way back from all over the country to the person who once had been a catalyst to what Joseph Campbell calls "the moment of aesthetic arrest when the possibility of a life of adventure is opened to the mind."

Perception—especially visual perception, in that moment when the spirit is tripped into awareness—guides the giving of our hearts, the choosing of how we spend the finite-infinite bit of time we all have allotted to us. In the words of the troubador (Guiraut de Bornelh), "The eyes are scouts of the heart, and the eyes go reconnoitering for what it would please the heart to possess. . . . " Time doesn't give too many second chances to such adaptable creatures as we. A lifetime spent in illustration may preclude one's becoming the painter that might have been. The creature has changed. And if the creature was curious and easily fascinated, the creature was snared for good.

Now many city libraries that nourished so many of us are at a crossroads, and at least three directions point to despair if help is not given them. Some ask if their work is drawing to an end in this audiovisual age. One feels like shouting, "No!" Perhaps different ways must be found to reach children, to give them the privacy to make their own choices of books, to roam freely in time and place. I wonder how many school libraries with little space have solved some of the problem of the need for a child to get off by himself with a beloved book.

Recently I visited one in Kansas in which an old-fashioned white bathtub with claw feet, filled with cushions, provided the coziness a window seat used to offer, and an ingenious principal had constructed a kind of tree house over the charging desk to serve the same purpose. If there are adults with imagination and ingenuity, able to remember the children they were, they will find ways to serve children, to give them a footing near the center of the wheel. Their sweet persuasion will leap from their hearts and minds to others.

Doesn't experience often mean that someone has been touched by beauty, pain, terror, exhilaration, and wishes—however he can—to make a clear sign to who comes after? "This is what I've found." "You come, too." Tell it, chant it, dance it, play it, paint it—life is infinitely precious. Find out for yourself—that is the message. Life is spread out like a banquet: toasts, delights, cautiously approached new flavors, revelations, initiations—there for the prepared and unprepared. But the meal cannot be digested if one is unprepared. The joy of the artist when he conceives the image jumps like a spark to the mind that apprehends it.

From all sides, we are all but asphyxiated by the mauve perfumes of nostalgia for a misunderstood past. It seems the fate of eras to be revived by people then too young to have experienced the real thing, if they were alive at all. These cycles of rediscovery possibly start with curiosity, a search for the milieu that formed and nourished our fathers and mothers. Sometimes they start in reaction to a present that is hard to take.

We have seen such a reaction in the past few years, a wholesale rollercoaster ride backwards fifty years in design, dress, bookmaking. And now that wave seems to be ebbing and there are many dazed and damp survivors bogged in the sand, the drumbeat that had pounded so insistently now only an echo. You all know them—these dripping survivors trying to fit their steps to a beat they had rejected, trying to find their own beat.

The rollercoaster didn't stop there. The tightly framed engravings of the Victorians crop up in our picture books. All the intervening progress in freeing the page from the tightness required by letterpress printing seems to be ignored for a manageable neatness. One skillful artist, working through his own loves and inner compulsions, can start a trend of Victoriana in style. Detail piles on detail and eventually, to quote from Lily Tomlin's Mrs. Beasley, "There are some things you can make so cleverly that it is virtually impossible for anyone to tell if you have talent or not."

Caught in a pattern perceived to be meaningless, spirits die. The old mythological symbols, often those a child will make in his earliest drawings, galvanize life, give the self a chance to recognize its drives, its evil as well as its good. Without even being aware of it, the developing spirit longs for some aspiration. The vans, campers, sun roofs fill the summer roads—away from the chemical and mechanical artificiality of much of our life, away to sea and sun and an illusion of being closer to the core of things.

Every once in a while, we get a glimpse of "the wild heart of life." We are often closest to its rhythmic beat in the ancient tales that have come from the past, tested again in other ages—teller and told eventually one. A thousand years of travel and translation into Persian, Greek, Hebrew, Latin, German, and French took the *Panchatantra* to La Fontaine. The beasts are still coherent. But many of these tales, honed by ages of living into pith, beat to a timeless heart rhythm. Heroes, like gods, wear many guises, and those who seek will find them. After a child looks at television five hours a day, his heroes are apt to be rather different from ours. Painful time and rare time when man reaches high to touch the moon's face and we can see it happen any place on earth in our own living rooms.

Out of a real time, a real place, real people, exploit becomes marvel, then legend, then a folktale. Out of dreams, longings, psychological imbalances, fantasies become fairy tales. You who work directly with children know that the best of many people has to pass through some crass channels in order to reach them and is often fortunate to reach them more or less intact. A short time ago, a friend brought home Godfried Boman's book of tales, translated from the Dutch: *The Wily Witch*—haunting, magical, and often somber tales, full of joy, but also clear-eyed in facing the sadness living brings. *The Rich Blackberry Picker* saw fields of jewels in the morning sun, great halls of pillars, with blue-and-white mosaic ceilings, and heard each dusk the voice of a marvelous singer. When the townsfolk who had heard tell of the wonders realize what they were, they hang the blackberry picker. And the record of that story is cracked.

Television—subtle, sustaining nursemaid to countless children—is giving them their beliefs, their values, and also prematurely jading their reactions. Travesties of traditional fairy tales, ridiculing the purity of the heroes' motives, intensifying excitement to the point of mania, destroy utterly patience for the pleasure in calmer treats. How tame, seen from now, were our struggles way back there for freedom to use dialect if that was the way a person spoke, to portray children even nude if the story demanded it. The mores of one age spill into another.

But what effect will all this passive viewing have on the urge to do for oneself—creativity, if you wish so to call it—that is formed in childhood? Play will imitate life, even if life is secondhand, adult, contrived, and crass. Will the child watcher be able to create pictures in his mind? What do our own illustrations do to his imaginings? One can never *decide,* by one's work, to involve a child's imagination and feeling. Only one's own involvement will live in the image for him.

Time—to explore, to question, to grow—time, and more effort than a flip of the dial. The misuse of power, the ridicule of age-old wisdom, the casualness about the worth of life, and the rewards of knowledge—piles of cash, cars, stoves, and TV's: What do we have to offer to balance all this? We have first ourselves and then our own belief that the myths that make fabulous time our time are worth telling. Chronological time ceases to have meaning when we are dealing with all or any time. The same old process of fantasy—to dream, to vision, to revelation about the world and about ourselves—goes on.

These simple little books? Yes—because in some small way man-as-child must be taught that his brother is not his prey. What we are trying to give children is some cache of inner life, some still point from which he can communicate with life through words, images, motions, colors, rhythms. Every once in a while, an artist or author, sometimes not even by intention, steps on the still point of that turning wheel where myths live eternal. We have all been through struggles before and certainly shall be again, but meanwhile, Buddha told this story:

"A traveler, fleeing the tiger chasing him, ran until he came to the edge of a cliff. There he caught hold of a thick vine and swung himself over the edge. Above him, the tiger snarled. Below him, he heard another snarl, and behold, there was another tiger peering up at him. The vine suspended him midway between two tigers. Two mice, a white mouse and a black mouse, began to gnaw at the vine. The traveler could see they were quickly eating it through. Then, in front of him on the cliffside, he saw a luscious bunch of grapes. Holding onto the vine with one hand, he reached and picked a grape with the other. How delicious!"

Every year, our little town of Redding, Connecticut, celebrates Labor Day weekend with a book fair that grows and grows and now assumes almost medieval proportions, for people come to it from miles around and take away books in their arms or in cardboard cartons sliding on the floor, gleams in their eyes because the books are bargains—gifts to the fair of used books that are resold to earn money for the library Mark Twain started by giving money himself and dunning weekend guests to his country retreat. But they take away a great deal more than books. The wheel turns very fast for children, slows up for the eager young-middle-aged and rushes again, headlong, for donors of the sometimes rare and lovely old editions that find their way there. Bargains, yes, but discoveries, old friends one has not been in touch with for years, and occasionally you will find a copy with an anonymous gift from time, a quotation, notes, personal proof of possession before it is passed on. In one of these—a paperback edition of Nancy Wilson Ross's *The World of Zen*—I found this quote from Morris L. West's *The Ambassador* (Morrow, 1965), copied in pencil on the half-title:

"Remember, what you seek is an 'inwardness.' It will give you no precise answer to the 'outwardness' in which you are involved. It will not show you how to succeed as an ambassador or to 'solve' one problem by changing it into another. What it will show you is that the secret of life and survival and betterment is carried on by the individual and not the man. So that whatever is done for the better in your work, or anyone's work, must be done by and through the inwardness of individual men."

In the words of the Zen master Hoyen: "When water is

scooped up in the hands, the moon is reflected in them; when flowers are handled, the scent soaks into the robe."

And now the merry-go-round stops briefly and I get on. How very proud and happy I am that you have let me join this company.

THE LOTUS BLOSSOM—OR WHO-DUN-IT?

*"We betray our children when we fail
to take a long view of their lives."*

I live with a friend who reads Ngaio Marsh, P.D. James, Dorothy Sayers, and Agatha Christie, with the greatest relish, for relaxation. My trouble is that I can't relax or even sleep if I do so. My Who-dun-its have to be of other deeds.

I'm first going to talk to you about an ugly subject, one that we all know about, perhaps have been part of, either as perpetrator or victim, but one that we can do something about. The subject is common to who-dun-its—betrayal.

The advantage of climbing is often the view one gets as one pauses on the way. The same might be said for sticking with a career over several decades. I don't have to tell you that this is a discouraging period. City library budgets allow an annual purchase of maybe 200 books. The closing down of children's literature classes or library schools themselves, indicates that with all our educational effort that has attained about 97% literacy in the country, a huge number of Americans are not

A speech given at the University of Oklahoma, Norman, Okla., on October 2, 1982.

reading. They have been given the name of aliterates—those who can but won't read, will turn quickly to the pictures. It might seem odd to you that this upsets an illustrator. But of course we are going to feel the effects of this aliteracy, even though the technology in part responsible can inform us, can entertain us, can even help us to earn a living with scant attention paid to reading. People who seldom read or write of course lose respect for precision of language. You have heard the mumbles and grunts as some otherwise attractive soul tried desperately to verbalize a thought. But ultimately one wonders if not reading may not come to mean not thinking clearly.

Not long ago Townsend Hoopes, president of the Association of American Publishers, was quoted in the New York *Times,* speaking of the dangers this problem poses for the nation. We are not a verbal culture with fabulous oral histories. "The inevitable consequence," he said, "is that such people [referring to aliterates] seem satisfied with their own initial, shallow interpretations of what they do read, and deeply resist requests or instructions to explain or defend their points of view with any reasoned analysis or cogency."

Ahead of us may lie a clearer than ever division in the country, a narrow elite of informed people and a large majority who cannot be bothered to read. You could take that further into the cruder designation of an almost feudal culture and call the divisions the exploiters and the exploited, or even eventually the knaves and the fools.

Three million young people get high-school diplomas in a year, but how many read? More than 98% of American homes have television, and here come Pac-Man, his wife, and all his friends.

There are many encouraging experiments being tried out in various parts of the country. In Connecticut, schools are

aware that children spend enormous numbers of hours looking at television, absorbing, along with much information, values, mores, points of view that have been manipulated for the
sake of viewer ratings. They have conducted experiments,
asking children not to look at any television at all for set
periods of time—say, two weeks. The results—no one can say
how long the effects will last—were surprising. Instead of
missing the programs, the children found that they had more
time for after-school outdoor play, for their own hobbies, and,
miraculously enough, for reading. Library circulation went up.

The shadow of the nuclear conflict is bringing about a more
and more narrow fundamentalism. To be secure about fun-
damentals is to live intact in a cocoonlike safety. Other arguments are closed out of the mind. But when all things are
certain, does not mental rigor mortis set in? We are seeing a
worldwide outbreak of fundamentalism—religious and political—as people yearn for certainties. Some paths lead to
Jonestowns. Some paths lead to a courageous summoning of
strengths, a sorting out of gear, to a determination not to be
seduced by terror and hatred—or to fall into an acquiescence
that ends in self-betrayal.

In our local newspaper the plans for mass evacuation to
Vermont are discussed, ludicrous as the evacuation of mega-
lopolis that is crippled by a four-inch snowfall may be, instead
of plans that have the courage to say, "No! This must not be."

Are ideas worth more than life? If there is no life, what
chance has the idea? If you do not know the book *Silence* by
the contemporary Japanese author, Shusaku Endo, I strongly
recommend it. Its message: What can be the real test of faith?
What is the ultimate moral act?

Another book has been called by Julian Symons of the London *Sunday Times,* "The most successful book yet written
about the greatest single horror inflicted by one group of men

upon another." It is *Black Rain,* by an elderly, unsentimental, and unsparing novelist, Masuji Ibuse. We are just beginning to get information about the long-term effects of the bombs dropped on Japan that were a fraction of the power of the bombs that could be used today.

In our town we have a book fair to benefit the library, which has always received its major funding from the interest and labors of the townspeople. Books are donated, sorted, and priced throughout the year and offered for sale Labor Day weekend. There is a Collector's Corner, an auction, the plum of which last year was a first edition of *Moby Dick.* The idea of books living many lives in many homes is delightful. The sight of booklovers going out hugging their boxes of purchases, often at prices below current paperback prices, is heartwarming. We happen to be a rather bookish community.

On Sunday afternoon, after three days of work on the fair, my friends and I knocked off and went on a picnic to a lovely pond in a local state park. Why do parks so often commemorate warlike encounters? The pond is full of Chinese lotus, great creamy white cups and huge leaves, that are changing form constantly, flopping this way and that in every breeze. The leaves, like many other things, are most interesting when they are nearing the ends of their lives, torn by winds, battered by autumn rains. Brown and ragged, they curl and droop over their now empty seedpods until they slip back into the mire to store up strength for next summer's blooming once more of that startling beauty and purity. One can understand why the Oriental civilizations revered the lotus as a symbol of spiritual power and rebirth. When the flower has finished blooming, the seedpods form—looking like medieval Venetian chimney pots—and the stalks lose their sinuousness and dry, eventually bending over and dropping the seeds into the mud.

That Sunday afternoon I took many photographs to which I can refer while painting. For some time I have been studying the Chinese technique of painting, learning the basic strokes derived from Chinese calligraphy, learning from observation of master paintings, trying to incorporate into a painting the opposites, Yang and Yin, that so long ago the Chinese were aware made up the richness of life, the smooth and scratchy, the sensuous flow and the rasping, dragged brush textures. The subject matter is modest, a slug swinging on a blade of grass, a flower half-hidden in leaves. But whatever one paints, it is the end of a contemplative process that began with looking, with feeling, associating the ephemeral with something more durable in the spirit, with thinking, with again, minute observation. A painting that is vital, vibrant with spontaneity, may be the last in a group of many that were not. The means are the simplest: ink from soot rubbed on stone, a brush of hair, paper from natural fibers. The very materials are part of one's feeling about the pictures. Like the daily practice of music, the daily practice of painting enables one to do the painting when the time comes, to perform as one would like.

As a people we often shy away from tackling the difficulties of learning an art or how to judge it. It is depressing to witness the floundering of reviewers who often do not seem to realize that a finished work is but the tip of an iceberg. What is not seen may be the months or years of thought and feeling from which the final work was distilled.

I have a young friend with an eagerness to draw who spends all her time making more or less accurate copies of Snoopy. She is no longer content with the expressionist paintings of her early childhood. In school she is encouraged into a facile, colorful design demanding neither imagination nor observation nor feeling, certainly very little muscular control. And so those muscles that helped so gaily to delineate her pleasures as a small child, go unused. Snoopy is safe and won't show up the wobbles and naïveté she now sees in her early pictures. He is blessedly the same, and so are her pictures; and a door is slowly closing, possibly forever, because a teacher refuses to, or doesn't know enough to, recognize the need for training muscles to respond to brain impulses. If my young friend is very strong in her determination, perhaps she can bridge the period when her critical sense has outstripped her skill. But I can't help feeling that she has been betrayed, as so many of our children are betrayed.

Muscles untrained are very hard to bring under control later on. But worse, a period when the foundation for skills that will later enrich adult life are laid down, has been neglected.

I am finding this out daily as I practice the flute, trying to get muscles to respond allegro or presto.

We take it for granted that a surgeon's scalpel will be guided by a mind trained for years before it descends to make an incision.

Yet in spite of a wide interest in art there is still an ingenuous faith that new work still springs forth from an artist's hand with little or no preparation. When someone asks me what next book I am working on, and I reply that I am painting, a look of disappointment usually comes to the person's face, because he had expected a factory production of bright new images, and in my case, usually in a different technique and superficial style from any other of my books. I have always thought books are as individual, or should be, as the people who make them. We all work differently. I have often wondered how an artist can keep on applying the same technique year after year to a vast number of different subjects. Is it laziness? Is it a habit of wishing to please that set in when he was young and shepherded through his first books by a strongminded editor? Is it simply an imperviousness to boredom that some of us feel if we do the same thing over and over? I don't know. Illustrators are a diverse lot! But after a few books, we are apt to know ourselves well enough to know what we need in the way of a long period without pressure, in which to grow, and more important, be receptive to ideas that spring up, as it were, from nowhere but in truth from the whole well of impressions and associations that we are feeding on every day. Some illustrators work under the closest direction from editors. If I feel one snuffling at the back of my neck, I go to pieces. We all know that publishing and distribution of books are different from what they were thirty years ago. Publishers quite frankly ask authors today, not only to write the book, but to sell it, and often push farther into the future or out of the window altogether the chance for the author to work undisturbed on his next. There are two sides to this question. Most of us welcome the opportunity to meet the people who use our books with children, and always return from some jaunt of speaking somewhat enriched from new human contacts. But we often wonder, also, if that is the best way to spend energy that as we get older is less, and more precious. In this situation, someone is sure to betray himself or someone else.

We betray our children when we fail to take a long view of their lives. Interest in the arts grows, yet in some schools children laboriously construct huge oilcloth hamburgers because some adult artist had success creating one. Swimming pools and arenas get built. The funds the libraries had got are now cut. When art is so accessible in the museums of our large cities, perhaps the reaction is, "The children can always be taken." Are they?

In some towns where art is not readily accessible, much more effort is made to teach children that art is something to live with, to make if you can, but a sustaining food for mind and imagination and spirit. Recently I visited a library in Oklahoma where valuable prints and sculpture circulated to the children along with their books, just to make sure they got that nourishment.

"Isn't gaiety one of the most important feelings to have in life?"

"No, joy."

Every time we opt for shallowness, every time we fail to exercise the muscles of deeper feelings, we betray our children.

Like many college students, I worked in the summer to help with my expenses. I got a job at a country inn, expensive for the time, to which came many people whose names were known to me from the art, music, and theatrical worlds. Exposure to strong individual personalities when one is young is priceless as a means of growth.

I wanted art lessons; so I offered to work for my training, sweeping studios, setting up huge still lifes from which we would select smaller groups on our canvases, timing the model's poses, all the chores necessary in an art studio that leave plenty of time to paint and learn.

I was blessed to be able to study under a gifted painter, Judson Smith, who was also a wise and compassionate man. Like many children I was brought up trusting in many certainties that, as I came to mature, I saw as illusions. The artist told me, "Try to be absolutely honest in your thinking for one minute." Can you?

He told me, "The only thing you can depend on is change."

Rather than deal in recipe methods that have to be discarded, he tried to bring out the fragment of uniqueness in each one of us.

"Find your grandfathers." Seek your own counterpoints of personality, cast of mind, in painters of the past. Learn from them, study them.

"The means, not the end." The daily practice, the hair-breadth progress that adds up in time to an inch, to a foot. The habit of taking responsibility for one's own slow growth. "Don't worry about a personal style. None of you is just like another." The caution about believing praise. The long view.

Young people can easily betray themselves. More easily are they betrayed by people who ask too little of them. When I am asked by a young person what he should do to prepare himself for a career in illustration, I am reluctant to suggest that he study with a fashionably successful illustrator. We all know what can be the result—as year after year the copies of the illustrator's style proliferate. A good foundation in felt drawing, painting with a painter who emphasizes observation and feeling for life, cultivation of a habit of drawing feelings, familiarity with as much great art as possible, analysis of composition, exposure to the other arts—music, dance, theatre—all these added to a familiarity with outstanding illustrated books to get a sense of how to handle a dramatic line, how to create and maintain characterization, the importance of extended research and the honest use of it as stimulus, not traceable model . . . the preparation will take years—many of them while practicing illustration. One is always preparing.

Techniques that fit the manner to the subject can be learned, invented as one goes along, if you are first convinced that such changes are necessary to your own growth.

An actor who used exactly the same voice and mannerisms for every character would be a sorry example of the breed, yet we happily look at endless pastel renderings, no matter what the country, the place, the period. Are we being betrayed? Are we betraying ourselves by asking too little?

Illustrators of my generation have been through many battles, have seen many styles come and go. In the forties, perhaps as a backwash from the grief and horror of World War II, there was a wash of sugary sentimentality akin to that of popular greeting cards. You know the style. You know the commercial success of such a style. You also know how pallid is such a view of childhood.

In the fifties some of the rigor of abstract-expressionism exploded in our books. In spite of almost constant war someplace in the world, it was a time of expansion, exploration, and discovery. Then in the sixties, someone—perhaps because he had seen the Art Nouveau Show and exhibition of Tiffany glass at the Museum of Modern Art, rediscovered the sinuous line. But the snakeskin was empty. The living creature was gone, in spite of a hundred Magic Markers.

In the seventies, many wanderers returned to safety, and the safety was someone else's.

From the confusion of growing up in the fifties, when drawing from life was not thought necessary and self-expression was all, young illustrators shot in the other direction, copying photographs in a deadly imitation of the look of things; and the spirit again was somehow missing. Antlike attention to every stitch in his pants does not a lively little boy portray. Illustrations became symbols, shorthand. Two chevrons were smiling eyes, one inverted chevron a smiling mouth. The nose was often lost in the shuffle. These facile symbols may be amusing but are utterly incapable of expressing a deep response to life. Who is betraying whom?

It isn't enough to complain or nod to the vocal complainers. What are we going to do? We can almost always do something. We can choose. If we only can buy 200 books, let them be strong ones that will live in the memory. We can ask publishers to retain some of the strong books of the past rather than let them go out of print for a weaker new version.

There has been a spate, a flood, of individual folktale and fairy-tale books. Rather than yet another flossy, glossy over-decorated edition, why not reorder Wanda Gág? Evaluate and reevaluate.

When authors and editors who have devoted lifetimes of application of talent, integrity of spirit to their work are treated by publishers as commodities and therefore expendable, who is betraying whom?

Publishers are in business. Many of the ills besetting business are theirs. It seems that finally they are beginning to realize that a passion for black figures and an MBA are not the only qualifications necessary. They embrace the Peter principle passionately, and the perfectly competent secretary becomes a third-rate editor.

As Jean Karl wrote in a recent issue of *Advocate* (University of Georgia) the criticism of many issues by parents' groups first shocked sturdy New Yorkers, used to endless variety in people and books. To act positively, she decided to be even more critical herself, and ask, "What is gratuitous, what is honestly necessary to characterization? What words are so necessary that the book is less without them? Are we going to betray children's need for diversity by settling for blandness?"

Willie, in the best of sashes,
Fell in the fire and burned to ashes.
After a while the room grew chilly.
But no one cared to stir up Willie.

A teacher in Arkansas told me recently that someone had stirred up Willie, having lost a sense of humor, and demanded that the anthology containing the offending verse be withdrawn from the library shelves.

Examples of loss of perspective and a sense of balance, even humor, abound, and I'm sure each of us has a tale to tell.

The leading characters change, but the play goes on, under

a different name— *Huckleberry Finn, Catcher in the Rye,* and now *Shadow.* You can name in your own minds the title for the next scene. Who will betray whom?

Reviewers of books sometimes measure the book in front of them against the book they had thought it would be or should be. They often don't even see the book in their hands for what it is. When we heed the words of critics who have looked at too much and felt too little, whom do we betray?

We can't pretend that 1980's children live in a Kate Green-away world, charming as that may be to have on our library shelves. Does anyone have to say again that unless we corrupt their taste by sugar or "strawberry shortcake," children are not sentimental creatures?

We betray children every time we act as if there is one way to do things, one way of feeling, one religion, one road to enlightenment. Experience, if we have learned anything at all, should have taught us otherwise.

One of the serendipities of that golden Sunday afternoon spent in contemplating the lotus was meeting Mitchell. Mitchell was three and had come to the park with his father and sister to fish. The sister and a young friend of mine went off to catch frogs. Mitchell felt his fish were taking too long to bite and walked around in search of company and conversation. But his conversation was measured in an original way. It all came out of his pocket.

"Where do you live?"

Deep delving into his shorts' pocket, a sidelong glance at the palm of his hand. "Bridgeport."

Every word he answered was brought forth from that pocket, examined, and then uttered with finality, like a card being slapped on a table.

"I have some surprise words," he finally offered.

"What are they?"

Deep into the pocket again. "Strawberry pie!"

Mitchell didn't know it, but in that pond he was a lotus seed.

SHADOW: THE VOICE OF ILLUSTRATION

*"In illustration for children we are trying
to stimulate an inner sort of viewing."*

Along with many other Americans, I am reading a delightful
book—*Blue Highways* by William Least Heat Moon, brother
to Little Heat Moon and son to Heat Moon. Talking of his
father, the author says, "It's a contention of Heat Moon's—
believing as he does any traveler who misses the journey
misses about all he's going to get—that a man becomes his
attentions. His observations and curiosity, they make and
remake him."

Many years ago, after I had taught high school English and
dramatics for three years, I decided to do what I really wanted
to do—paint and try to work on children's books. I knew very
little about them, so I got a job as a library assistant in the New
York Public Library. My first library was on the Lower East Side
of New York in a Russian-Ukrainian section, where many people were immigrants or first generation Americans. I started
doing storytelling and was transferred to the Central Chil-

A speech given at the University of Georgia, Athens, Ga., May 1983. Published in *The Advocate,* October 1983.

dren's Room, where I worked for the next five years, storytelling, helping to put up exhibitions that were always tied to
the books in the collection but which stretched children's
minds beyond their everyday world. I worked with a very
valuable old book collection and of course learned everything
I could about library work. It was a wonderful way for a young
person to get acquainted with the best books available in
English for children and the children from all over the city who
used them, and also the foreign language books in a collection
that was used by children from other countries, but also by
editors, authors, illustrators, and designers.

On a shelf behind the Reading Room desk was a small book
that intrigued me. It had a title we would not give such a book
today, *Petits Contes Nègres pour les Enfants des Blancs,* by the
French poet Blaise Cendrars, published in France in 1929.
Margery Bianco translated all but one of the stories and called
her book *Little Black Stories for Little White Children.* The book
was published in 1933. I learned some of the stories in that
collection and told them in my story hours. They were powerful and mysterious, and the children liked them. The one
story-poem that Margery Bianco did not translate was called
"Le Féticheuse," or "The Sorceress." I read it in the French
and heard Maria Cimino tell the story to adults in the translation of her husband, Will Lipkind.

Not too long ago, I watched and listened, on Public Television, to Monteverdi's *The Coronation of Poppaea,* directed
by Pierre Ponelle. It occurred to me that the tempo of a film
is very much like the tempo of music and also of pictures.
There are broad, slow rhythms, staccato rhythms; the rhythms
grow out of the mood and also help set it.

I had been haunted by the mood of that one story-poem by
Cendrars that I had come to call *Shadow* in my mind and

decided to try to make pictures for it that could incorporate some of my feelings about it.

I would like to think of some of my books as not ending with themselves but setting up resonances, echoes and reechoes, changes on the theme.

Whether people refer to *Shadow* as a story or not, I do not feel it is a story in the usual sense but a prose poem. Illustrating a poem is very different from illustrating a story. A story usually has a rising dramatic line, a definite climax, a falling off of action before being tied up at the end.

Shadow was quite different. There is no plot line, but there is a buildup of intensity. Each episode creates its own mood that contributes to the overall effect of mystery; and the line then returns at the end to the eye of the child and the dance of light in the pupil.

The poetic mind thinks in metaphor. It sees intuitively the connection that flashes illumination back and forth between things. The illustrator often delineates images in metaphor and by means of color and dynamic action intensifies meaning.

The poem *Shadow* makes use of repetition—a kind of refrain: "It does not cry out. It has no voice." Repetition is a favorite device of storytellers the world over, but especially in Africa. The phrase emphasizes the silence; it causes the reader or listener to pause in midthought.

Harold Scheub, in a paper published by the University of Wisconsin in 1969, describes storytelling performances in the Transkei by a Zulu teller, sometimes male, sometimes female. The story is told at dusk, before children go to bed. "No light except that cast by the fire, and the performer, through a skillful use of repetition and rhythm, gesture and song, almost hypnotizes the children, her movements rendered phantasmagorical as the flames and shadows created by the fire play

165

on her face and body." The basic element of such a performance is a core cliché, a song, chant, or saying expanded throughout the narration. The focus of such a *ntsomi* performance is the image; at the center of the image is the cliché. A repeated motion mesmerizes the audience and leads it almost physically to the conclusion.

Illustrators probably betray themselves when they try to explain what they did after they have done it. To try to put into words what was conceived in images can mean an almost complete about-face. A few years ago, I felt that what I could say might not have any meaning any longer for anyone. All of us possibly share these big landmark feelings that in some ways bind us more closely than ever to our humanness—death, loss, the recognition of limits. One realizes that older people have always shared some such feeling. The realization is liberating. One makes the decision to tap inner feelings and most blessedly not *care* what people think but to trust that they will feel what one is trying to communicate, whether or not they can articulate their feelings.

And then there are the critics: Some are acute, aware. Some are too young to have any memory of a former greatness; they try to discuss from hearsay. Some are too lazy to research truth. Some are too filled with their own present to put the past in its own historical perspective. Some do not understand the causes they embrace and flail wildly and widely, doing great harm.

Dr. Hubert Abrahamsohn, a psychologist from Düsseldorf who worked with the pianist Claudio Arrau, told him, "The less vain you become, the more creative you are. One gets to the point where one is courageous enough to displease."

In illustrating for children, we are trying to stimulate an inner sort of viewing. So much of childhood should be invested in memory. After a while we realize that only that work in which the artist and author went beyond pleasing, went farther along those mysterious inner passages of the mind, will provide an intense enough experience to live in someone else's memory. The experience of beauty, the excitement, electrification of the brain tissues, vibrating with new connections, new intuitions—doesn't it cry out to be shared?

We all work in shadow—parents, teachers, friends, editors, all looking over our shoulders. It takes years to learn to trust them with our real selves. When I decided to work on the poem I called *Shadow,* I decided to trust a variety of feelings it evoked in me. I knew the book would fail, at least for me, if I used realistic figures with realistic shadows. The metaphor of the silhouette is not for "blackness"—the animals are also black—but for a generalization. Black contains all colors, is the well where all mixtures end. Likewise, figuratively, all colors can be distilled from black. In Africa, white, the color of ash, is often the symbol not only of death but also of life in death—spirit.

The Fang mask of a girl from Gabon was kept on a family shrine containing the bones of the ancestor.

Shadow—so-called real shadow—is blue-purple, to point out its omnipresence.

Brilliant color would be in the setting rather than in the figures. A kind of continuity is expressed in both.

Dr. Yashiro Yukio, quoted by Yasunari Kawabata in his Nobel acceptance speech, *Japan the Beautiful and Myself,* summed up one of the special characteristics of Japanese art and of the poetic spirit of other art as well in one sentence: "The time of snows, of the moon, of the blossoms—then more than ever we think of our comrades." Could I add the times of Shadow to such a group?

Blaise Cendrars was an unusual and interesting man. He was born Frederic-Louis Sauser at Le Chaux-de-Fonds in the canton of Neuchâtel, Switzerland in 1887. His friend, the painter Sophia Delaunay, spoke of him as a self-invented personality, who liked to mix fantasy and reality. He was a vagabond, traveling from the Urals and the Orient to South America, Vancouver, and the United States, sometimes as a bodyguard, sometimes as companion to a splendidly eccentric gem dealer. A tough, inventive natural poet, he had great feeling and profundity and a passion for life. He was very much interested in painting as a form of poetry, the related rhythms similar to those of speech.

Cendrars spent a good deal of time in Africa and listened to storytellers and shamans before the evening fires. His story-poem of *Shadow* shows his fondness for playing with a theme. It mixes a child's perception of Shadow:

It comes sliding right up
behind the storyteller . . .
In the daytime
Shadow is full of life.
It waves with the grasses,
curls up at the foot of trees . . .
races with the animals
at their swiftest . . .

with a much deeper meaning of Shadow in much of Africa— the everconstant spirit of the ancestors, those who have gone before and given the group its character and ideals.

Little children would listen with their elders to a village story-teller at the ritualistic ceremonies not very much different in intent from many of our yearly ceremonies, when we take stock of who we are, what we came from, what we believe. Often the tales told to children were animal stories in which storytellers passed on to their listeners the lore of the social group, the wit and wisdom acquired by living. As Jamake Highwater says in his book *Dance,* "Ritual is not a product of primitive people. Rather, it is produced by peoples still in touch with the capacity to express themselves in metaphor." It is a way of dealing with forces beyond our control.

I think Cendrars knew exactly what was fact and what was fantasy. I do not think he had any idea of recording an actual piece of ethnic literature in *Shadow.* I had no intention of portraying modern Africa, since that was not what he had seen and felt.

A translator has an obligation not to change the intent of an author's text. In a way, an illustrator has the same obligation toward what she understands to be the meaning and intent of a text.

Scientists are practically sure that Homo sapiens evolved in Africa near the Equator, in the savannah country of Northern Kenya and Southwest Ethiopia. At one time a great lake filled the Great Rift Valley. Millions of years of sediment deposited by the river Omo, which meanders through the valley, hold secrets about our earliest ancestors that are just beginning to come to light. Volcanic ash, layers of silt, one stratum after another, were laid down. It is a land of cataclysmic geological upheaval, resembling somewhat some of the landscapes in Utah and Arizona.

I took a trip to East Africa in 1975. One of the strongest impressions I received from the land was a kind of timelessness, where animals obeyed the urge to hunt in order to eat and raise their young. Every animal, except the huge hippopotamuses and elephants, was both hunter and prey. Everywhere there were vultures, huge birds that feed on carrion, a common sight in all torrid countries. The people were mostly herdsmen with large flocks of cattle that they guarded with spears because there were no barriers between grazing lands and the hunting grounds of jackals, cheetahs, and lions. They were proud and beautiful people, dressed in a simple blanket of red ochre. Understandably, the people wished to keep their grazing lands, but the government had a responsibility to those already living in towns and wanted the land for crops. I saw hundreds and hundreds of elephants, some in areas that could hardly support their appetite for the trees that could not grow fast enough to provide the food they need.

The villages that I suggested in *Shadow* were the groups of circular huts typical of rural Africa that I had seen and visited in Kenya. The dancers were suggested by the magnificent photographs of Michel Huet, who photographed dance rituals in Africa for years to preserve a record before they should pass out of memory. I saw many kinds of dances performed by students from various ethnic groups in Kenya, who wished to preserve a heritage of which they were proud.

Africa is a vast continent of many peoples, languages, and dialects. I feel that it is well-nigh impossible to portray honestly its diversity in one book or to portray a part and then label it "This is Africa."

Although the poem suggests an African background, a reverence for the past, I felt that *Shadow* could say something to an American child, any child, regardless of color.

Poetry means different things to different people and is probably best illustrated in the mind of the reader. There is a great danger in being too literal and ending in limiting the imagination you had wanted to stimulate. When I started to think about illustrations for *Shadow*, I knew I must simplify certain elements. I decided to portray no special group but to range as freely as I felt did the imagination of the poet. I spent several months drawing myself into the material, painting black ink silhouettes of people at their daily life. I thought of various media that were possible. At one time I thought I might use photography with a trained dancer to dance out the various aspects and episodes of *Shadow*. Then I thought of woodcuts. I think of black African carvers as probably the best wood sculptors of the world. Their carvings of figures, of masks, are among the great works of art of the world, even though the purpose of these disciplined works by locally known carvers was not art for art's sake but tools for propitiation and ritual.

To the pastoral and agricultural societies of black Africa, Nature is a vital force. When it is violated by exploitation, by killing, it has to be replenished. Ritual ceremonies of dance, storytelling, and song bring together the whole community in this regeneration and replenishment of energy. Masks on humans completely hidden in special costumes signify the presence of the guiding spirits in the vessel—the wearer of the mask.

Even though, of course, I recognized that the illustrations in a child's book could not be compared with the great figures we see in our museums, I thought some cut medium might suggest the cleanness of line, subtlety of surface treatment, and possibly some of the power of the originals. I had trouble with my hands and did not feel that they could stand the strain of cutting the number of blocks needed for a forty-page, four-color book. I decided to use black cut-paper shapes, emphasizing gesture only, for the people and the animals, in order to unify the many episodes of the book. I experimented with different grays and finally decided on a blue-purple, the color of shadows I often saw in Africa at dusk, for the real shadows.

For the spirit shadows, ancestral images and masks and ghosts, the spirits of the dead, important to the meaning of the poem, I carved blocks and printed them on translucent tissue that I pasted to the acrylic-washed backgrounds. Occasionally I used a negative image, as I did when the child awakens in the night and is startled by the thought, "What if I am not here!" The backgrounds of the second half of the book were built up from bits of blotted, pasted paper.

Although the poem speaks of no particular child, I use the little girl stepping out of her shadow on the title page in other parts of the book. When Shadow is heavy when night falls, the little girl reaches out to touch the old man grieving for his lost sons, the warrior and the hunter. She is one of the children sitting on the rock, watching men follow the ghost of a former warrior into war, and it is in her eye that the pupil dances at the end of the book.

Some African urban areas are as sophisticated as any on earth; some people live in simple village societies, with raising millet their chief occupation; some are nomadic herdsmen.

Although the poem comes from an African inspiration, I believe it is a poem for anyone. It deals with the mystery behind our birth, stretching far into the past, the handing down of wisdom from older to younger; it deals with all children's fear of the dark and their pleasure at playing with their shadows. It deals with loss, with past ideals that can guide us but can also lead us into old, habitual responses such as war. These experiences are common to all.

It was in that spirit that I made the book. If he had not been taught to feel differently, would a black American child feel some resonance from the past? I don't know. Children so often accept our adult point of view toward what we give them. A sensitive librarian can easily lead children to think of the more subjective shadows in all our lives.

We all see things only with our own eyes. What may seem to be a stereotype to some, to others is not at all. *Shadow* is banned from school libraries in Boston. Augusta Baker, who has used the book widely with black children in the South and with young black student teachers, has told me of their pleasure in the book because it is *not* filled with stereotypes for them.

The Western world, where technique often replaces conviction, is all too happy to exploit modern Africa for gain, as it did the earlier Africa, although perhaps not so obviously. Is this the only African heritage we wish to pass on to children?

We are gradually learning to see that in earlier people there was wisdom in living in harmony with Nature. As our life becomes more and more complex, we need that wisdom.

Can we teach children to have pride in a past that merits study in order to learn from it? Few of us today, unless our parents and theirs before them were very careful of family records, can trace our forebears back beyond a handful of generations. Much of our heritage is a kind of mystery. Present-day Americans, unless they are first or second generation immigrants, all have to study freshly their origins in the past. No group possesses a priority on knowledge if all must study, travel, do research. This kind of informational knowledge can hardly be transmitted in our genes, much as we would like to identify with the achievements of our ancestors. History must be studied.

Instead of encouraging children to ignore that past or, worse, feel shame in it, would it not be better to encourage them to look back over their shoulders as they step away from their shadows?

SHADOWS

"What the arm cannot do, wisdom can."
(African proverb)

Of course, this is a very happy occasion for me, and I am grateful to all of you here and not here who have made it possible. I suspect it took a certain courage for those on the Caldecott selection committee to choose *Shadow* for a third medal. I am grateful for their courage.

My publisher, Charles Scribner, Jr., has trusted me through work on quite a few books by now, and especially on this one. Monica Brown Lamontagne, production manager at Scribners, by her integrity and her acute eye on proofs and press, assured the look I had hoped for. Dai Nippon of Japan printed it beautifully. Olga Richmond, the designer, and David Toberisky gave it their meticulous care. Lee Deadrick, then my editor, from the beginning of my interest in Blaise Cendrars's prose poem, believed in the book and had the grace and kindness to put no impossible pressure on me while I allowed it to grow. And I am more grateful than I can ever express to close friends—they know who they are—who stood by me during

Caldecott Medal acceptance speech given at the annual conference of the American Library Association in Los Angeles, Calif., on June 28, 1983. Published in *The Horn Book,* August 1983.

a painful hiatus in my work on *Shadow* and by their faith in me and the book enabled me to finish it in strength.

I am especially happy that my being here coincides with your reestablishing this ceremony as a banquet; so once again we break bread together. I have attended several of these occasions—some up here, some down there. Wherever one is, one cannot help but feel on this night a sense of celebration and pride that we are all somehow one in work very much worth doing, despite occasional "weary dismals" during the year.

A long time ago I found, in Italy, a little book of proverbs collected from various peoples of black Africa. Their pithy pertinence can leaven my words.

Proverb: "It's true that I killed an elephant; however, it's not true that I carried him home on my shoulders."

Have you looked down from a high hill or tower on traffic patterns around a well-engineered intersection? Drivers trust each other; they trust their own ability to drive and react quickly. They trust the reactions of their own machines. There are remarkably few accidents, considering the number of vehicles on the roads. They all seem held, as it were, in orbit by invisible threads of trust.

Proverb: "The tongue is a lion; if you let it run free, it will eat you up."

Illustrators often find themselves in an ironical position. Much of what they say about their work has to be after the fact because they think in images, not in words. Yet if they can't talk, heaven help them!

Proverb: "When you hear a good talker, don't agree with him all at once. What is hiding in the corner has not come out yet."

Many years ago, when I was a storyteller in The New York Public Library, I was fascinated by a little book in the French collection of the Central Children's Room: *Petits Contes Nègres pour les Enfants des Blancs,* published in France in 1929, with semiabstract and somewhat sophisticated illustrations. Margery Bianco translated that book and published, in 1933, *Little Black Stories for Little White Children* (Payson & Clarke), with handsome woodcut illustrations that suggested African wood carvings. The one piece in the French of Blaise Cendrars that Mrs. Bianco did not translate was "Le Féticheuse" or "The Sorceress."

I have been haunted for years by the mysterious atmosphere created by Blaise Cendrars as he evoked Shadow, a spirit coming to life in firelight, wandering in and out of memory, taking part in rituals that gave meaning to life, at times a mirror image of life.

Although the poem had been told more often to adults than to children (hauntingly, by Maria Cimino of The New York Public Library's Central Children's Room), I felt that in the 1980s the prose poem might have meaning for American children. Levels of awareness might be probed that might not have been reached so easily in 1933. We have grown, and we have also suffered a great deal, since 1933. Perhaps we have learned something about ourselves.

A trip to East Africa in 1975 showed me a land of dazzling light that carved bold shapes relentlessly against mysterious shadow, colorful rocks still displaying the scars of the geological upheavals that had formed them, savannahs of golden grasses, and brilliant sunsets before the sudden fall of night.

179

Proud peoples seemed caught between past and present. Magnificent animals were both hunters and prey. The shadow of scavengers hung greedy over the burning land.

One of my strongest impressions was of timelessness, a kind of innocence in which man lived with nature in a way barely imagined by Western man.

My challenge, if I were to make a book of "Shadow," as I had come to call the poem to myself, would be to incorporate the images that had formed in my head from reading the poem with impressions gained from travel in Africa, with records of anthropologists who had very recently tried to record ways of life that are constantly changing and absorbing influences from other societies and, in some cases, are disappearing altogether.

I recognized another challenge: to suggest the element of play with an idea that is implied in the text. I do not think that Cendrars ever imagined himself to be recording a piece of ethnic literature—even though *Shadow* is told in a form suggestive of some kinds of storytelling prevalent in Africa— any more than Picasso's *Les Demoiselles d'Avignon,* incorporating impressions of African masks, professed to be a record of those masks. It was a new creation. *Shadow* was in no way to be a documentary performance. Poets, children, and artists often delight in mixing the real and the unreal, intuitively aware that each feeds an understanding of the other. I trusted children to understand many more emotional levels of shadow than the obvious.

Cendrars, and that was not his real name, was in Africa over fifty years ago. He wrote of people living in pastoral and agricultural societies where Nature was beneficent but had to be appeased by ritual for the loss of vital forces taken from the earth. The explosive energy of dance, of song, of storytelling, of all the components of ritualistic ceremonies in which the

180

whole community shared, restored these vital forces, and equilibrium was maintained.

Proverb: "No matter how calm the lake, in it there may be crocodiles."

I was quite aware of the possible nonacceptance of the book on an African subject because I am white. Also, the book, as I had conceived it, would be very expensive to print and produce properly. I gave my publisher every chance to be released from our agreement. Scribners decided to trust me and gave me possibly the best printing of all my books, one that united tonalities that had been executed over many months, with a long interruption in between.

Proverb: "If you have tried in vain to fish with the sea low, try to fish at high tide."

I wanted to make the book as vivid as I could, to speak to any child, regardless of color. We all share fear, discovery, loss, and a sense of play.

At one time, I toyed with the idea of photography as a medium for *Shadow.* I would work with images created by a trained dancer. The book would have been very different. I decided to work out my own images. At one time, I had hoped to cut wood blocks for the pictures. Arthritic pain in my hands forbade that. I think of African wood-carvers as sculptors the peers of any in the world, regardless of the original purpose of their carvings—not as works of art in the sense that we enjoy them in museums but as tools of ritual with enormous spiritual and evocative power.

The text was a poem. Black, stark cut-paper figures for people and animals could unify its many episodes and avoid the individualization of character that would limit imagination. I used the deep violet-blue shadows I had seen at dusk in Africa to suggest actual shadows. I cut wood blocks and printed them in white on translucent paper to suggest memories, spirit-images, and ghosts. The round-headed Fang masks suggest that one newborn may be closest to his ancestors. A community consists of the ancestors, the living, and those yet unborn.

When I had completed half the illustrations, I was forced to stop work for a year because of illness. I later worked out the method of blotting to suggest a land scarred by the history locked in its rocks. Fragments of blotted paper were pasted together to build up the landscapes I remembered.

I conceived the book as a kind of day that starts with sunset, moving into night. Probably because of the huge clouds of dust kicked up by running animals, sunsets in Africa can be awesomely brilliant before a brief dusk. The book moves through another day and ends again with the fire that brings Shadow to life.

Since the book was not to be a literal record, I did not wish to limit it to any one group. Clothing in temperatures that can easily hover near 125 degrees Fahrenheit is apt to be minimal, but I also wished to show gesture as probably the most vivid mode of communication among the various members of the human family. Bodily positions were suggested by my own numerous photographs taken in Africa, by recent photographs taken by Leni Riefenstahl of the Kau and Nuba peoples, and those of Michel Huet, who spent years recording dance rituals of many ethnic groups in Africa before they would pass from memory.

Proverb: "A beautiful neck has no need of a pearl necklace."

Translation is not retelling. I decry and fear the growing tendency to think that a translator has the right to change thought, intent, or style. I made my own translation, telling it over and over to myself, keeping in mind the shifting image of a wonderful dancer-storyteller, images darting from her pointed fingers.

When I read *Shadow* to Lee Deadrick, she immediately thought it could speak to children. We were a bit optimistic in thinking that French editors would be more careful of old records than we sometimes are. It took Lee and her staff almost a year of writing back and forth to France before we were able to ascertain ownership of rights and go ahead.

Proverb: "Children sing the song which they hear from their mother and father."

We know, from the child deep within ourselves, that children rarely speak of all they feel. We often violate their privacy and urge them to expose inner feelings that are withered in our scrutiny. I have often trusted children to accept poetic truth when their elders were worried and confused by terminology unfamiliar to them or were too literal of mind. There are levels of response in children we often make no attempt to reach, so anxious are we to cram their small skins full of practical skills and information. We push them out of a time of precious reverie and inner growth at the price of stunted and shallow adult inner life. Worse, we are sometimes guilty of passing on to them fears, hates, all the baggage of our own pain, when there is often no need. One generation of twenty years can change mental climate a good deal.

Proverb: "Today and tomorrow are not the same thing."

The book was to be published as a children's book. Even though I never thought it for very young children, I felt that children would expect to find children in the illustrations. Along with dance, storytelling was often part of a ritual ceremony taking place in an open space in the village, attended

183

by the inhabitants, old and young. I showed an audience of children for the storyteller, who tells his animal tales and passes along to his listeners the lore and wisdom of their society.

Shadow is often paradoxical. Playing with his idea, Cendrars moves back and forth between the shadow seen and known to the child as playmate, an accompaniment to all that lives in light, and shadow unseen, the ancestral past, the spirit that lives after life, after light, after fires are quenched. In no way did I wish to make a literal picture of African life, and indeed what picture book could undertake to show honestly the incredible diversity of a huge continent? Customs of pastoral peoples are not those of the forest, still less those of the cities that have grown so remarkably in the last half century. I would have to range as freely as the poet.

On the title page, a child steps out of her shadow, giving a backward look to the powerful ancestral images of the past. Some of the strongest possible means for instilling awe and reverence for ancestral spirits are the ritual dance masks. They absorb and control an energy released by the death of living creatures and make that energy available as a good, rather than as a surrender to chaos. When making the Bwa mask from Upper Volta, I worked until that mysterious transferal of spirit could take place, the leap from the spirit of the artist into the thing created. The evocation of spirit existing in the husk of an artist's creation is unmistakable when it occurs, the result of concentration and utter submergence of mind into material.

A child awakens in the night, perhaps for the first time startled at the thought, "What if I am not?" and feels the hole of nothingness, the negative of all positive.

In Africa, as Joseph Campbell has written, "Ash is the key

to the sacred." Ash, what is left after fire, after growth, after purification, becomes the eyes of Shadow.

A child lifts a stone and uncovers shadow people squirming in the shock of light. A boy child, who had danced so gaily at noon, is lost. Shadow sits heavy on the heart in the evening, as a child seeks to comfort the grandfather who has lost his hunter son, his warrior son. And the poet sings with his lute to their joy, sings to their grief.

Proverb: "If a village burns, all see the smoke; but if the heart is in flames, no one notices."

Years ago, I told some of Cendrars's stories to children. I knew their power. My first chance to use my book *Shadow* with children came last year before it was published. I showed slides of my pictures and read the poem aloud to a second-grade class in a public school in a nearby town. The children were of many nationalities, many colors—half of them boat people from Laos, Cambodia, and Vietnam. Many had recently lost family members. Some were gifted in art, such as Phovanh Mekmorakoth from Laos, whose picture of a blackbird among little yellow-green orchids hangs on my studio wall; Eddie Pacific, who wrote, "Were we excellent when we read our stories?"; Ruth Ashby, who wrote, "You told us we were casting a shadow on you. You will remember us, won't you?"; and Paul Arbitelle, who wrote, "I'd like to be an artist because it's peace." As I read, shadows flickered over their faces.

Proverb: "Fruits do not shake off by themselves; someone is under the tree."

Vituperations tell a great deal more about those who utter them than about the work attacked. Self-appointed experts are often people who are distinguished—for their ignorance as well as for their arrogance. Their eagerness to take up cudgels for causes they appear barely to understand often seems to be purely careerist in intent. They need not concern us here, and their words had best be forgotten. My concern is for the people who do have an emotional stake in conflicts that confront us, who have suffered real pain and understandably do not wish the children they teach to suffer the same pain. They feel a passionate responsibility to protect children from stigma that is unjust. I would hope that they might also interpret their responsibility as one of leading children away from facile, indignant labels of stereotype into a feeling of pride in a distant background of which we are just beginning to perceive the worth.

Works of art from this background have proudly taken their place all over the world. Were they fashioned by so-called primitive people, these exquisite and powerful objects, with such subtlety and finesse of surface, with the inner power only true works of art possess? I think not. Regardless of whatever fad in art is having its heyday, art history has sifted out those works endowed with spirit, not photographic finish or the product of antlike copying of nature.

Western man, in his arrogance, has left a wake of bruised peoples around the world. The seeking of power demands a putting down to build oneself up.

We are learning that what might have appeared, long ago, to be a meager spiritual and physical diet was far more sound than the endlessly diluted, manipulated fare we sometimes put up with because we think we have no control over it. In the paradox that psychology has taught us to recognize, Western man has envied the wealth of those he chose to label primitive, feared them because their lives were different, and eventually hated them because he had mistreated them.

Proverb: "What the arm cannot do, wisdom can."

We are now in a position of learning wisdom from people we had been taught to think of as primitive. Could children nearer in heritage to those roots be taught pride in them? Many of the rest of us bear in our heritage the shame of what might merit the words *bestial,* even *satanic*—certainly *inhuman.*

Proverb: "A drop of water can be the beginning of a deluge."

Why must we cling to the mental fix that an idea presented to a child be law forever after? Why is one example immediately frozen into an archetype? Or a stereotype? Do we really understand just what that word means? Where do our clichés come from, if not from fact?

Proverb: "A lie can produce flowers, but not fruit."

How are we to enable children to explore different modes of thinking and feeling if we exclude what we, in our literalness, cannot accept? There are those with wounds still open, from hurts some of us can hardly imagine, who are hypersensitive to any wind that seems harsh to barely healing flesh. Their expressions of dismay are honest. I ask them for their trust.

Proverb: "He who keeps asking and asking will not get lost."

Last year Julia MacRae published for Franklin Watts a beautiful and unaffectedly wise book by a great artist, the singer Janet Baker. It is a journal of her last year of singing in opera. Translate for yourselves her references to listening into those of looking:

The power of art is a person-to-person communication. It is meant for one ear, one heart at a time; one's own. What is received is unique, and cannot be got vicariously from listening to the remarks or the opinions of others. One must drink at the life-giving fountain for oneself. What is tasted there depends upon the individual.

For us, the performers, another sort of life-and-death struggle is going on. Our concern is how well we have prepared ourselves to do the job, mentally, physically, spiritually. Only we can know this, and even then, partially; all we can do is try our best at a particular moment, but it must be the best, nothing less.

Proverb: "Tasting the fruit, think with gratitude of who planted the tree."

Politicians and their ambitions notwithstanding, the more we learn of the mythologies of the world, the more we learn of the one creature, man. The great themes of his fears, his imaginings, his worship are legion and universal. As Joseph Campbell says in the prologue to his first volume in *The Masks of God* series, *Primitive Mythology* (Viking):

"and though many who bow with closed eyes in the sanctuaries of their own tradition rationally scrutinize and disqualify the sacraments of others, an honest comparison immediately reveals that all have been built from one fund of mythological motifs—variously selected, organized, interpreted, and ritualized, according to local need, but revered by every people on earth."

Come down from the height and watch the cars—Cougars, Sky Hawks, Thunderbirds, Cobras, and Rabbits. We still keep our totemic distinctions. We are still tribal in our allegiances, in our exclusions from our own state of blessedness, and in our mistrust of those we exclude.

We are entering a period forecast hundreds of years ago, one that will probably be cerebral, calculated, terribly competitive for material gain or material survival, depending upon who and where you are. A great deal that is very precious to us may mean next to nothing to this coming generation and those following. But our joy must be in going forward, trusting each other and the children we serve, sharing the common purpose of recognizing the spark of life that can ignite and nourish spirit. Isn't that why we are here? Africa is slowly stepping out of its shadows. Isn't it time that we stepped out of our shadows?

THERE'S SOMETHING IN
THE AIR

*"Our work can give birth to change, can touch, heal,
comfort or bring joy to the human heart."*
(from *Full Circle* by Janet Baker)

When Barbara Rollock asked me to speak to you today in
the name of a great and dear lady who was a legend in her
own time and—though she was no longer in charge of work
with children in the New York Public Library system—was still
a very lively force in that work, I was very much honored and
was immediately engulfed in a rush of memories. I hope you
will bear with me if I share some of them with you.

I knew Anne Carroll Moore when I was young and still form-
ing an inner credo— as a friend, not as a supervisor. I am
lucky to be able to sort fact from legend, with memory. This
woman from Maine, single-minded in the way genius can be,
planted an incandescent ideal in the minds of those who
worked with her—an ideal that they, in turn, would pass on
to others.

Unfortunately, I never knew the dynamic younger woman,

Anne Carroll Moore Lecture, given at the New York Public Library on May 21,
1984.

193

who, as she told me, thought nothing of walking eighteen miles a day in the English lake country to harden up her body after a severe attack of pneumonia. At the time I knew Miss Moore, I lived just below Washington Square. Then she was working on *The Art of Beatrix Potter*. I might get a call at any moment: "Come on over and see what Mr. Lindner has sent this time," and we would pore over the exquisite little watercolors of that other so dearly obsessed woman who was her friend.

I received many kindnesses from Nicholas, the little Dutch figure whose story Miss Moore told in *Nicholas—A Manhattan Christmas Story* and *Nicholas and the Golden Goose*. I know many children loved Nicholas's books, but I was almost more drawn to the little wooden figure and his treasure—tiny tools that all worked, a crystal ball, little golden Russian Easter eggs from Nadia Rodzianko—than I was to the fantasies that I found somewhat artificial.

Many people had difficulty in accepting Nicholas for what he was because they tried to pen him into an image limited by their own imaginations and facile attempts to read psychological meanings into what seemed to them a substitute child. If Miss Moore knew of these attempts, she may have been amused, or she may have been dismayed or even hurt. Virginia Mathews told me of a conversation she had with Anne Carroll Moore not long after the second, very attractive little figure of Nicholas had been left in a taxi on her way up to the apartment Helen Masten and I shared on 96th Street. The sturdy little carving in his homespun clothes, who had charmed so many children, I hope fell into the hands of one child for his special delight. We never heard. Miss Moore told Virginia that Nicholas had been for her a kind of touchstone for sizing up people, since their reactions told her much about their sense of play and their ability to enter a child's world, with its love of miniatures. "It's a game, really," she said.

I felt that Nicholas was an alter ego for part of herself, somehow, identifying with those sturdy Dutchmen in the Knickerbockers. He was also a means for permitting a sensitive woman, who knew her young guests had no way of repaying his invitations in kind, the delicacy of removing from them a sense of obligation. "He enjoys it," she would say, and indeed he had excellent taste in restaurants and was a gallant host.

On special gift-giving occasions, Nicholas would part with some exquisite treasures of his, such as a tiny *Histoire de Polichinelle,* with beautiful engravings, bought many years ago in France. But Nicholas also often seemed to embody the eternal spirit of childhood.

Poor Barbara Rollock! Could she have known what she asked? Or what I, in a temporary flush of confidence that I might have something worthwhile to say to you, was agreeing to? Because after a year of concentration on images, many of them Chinese, and some musical notes, I have not been thinking in words. But there is one word that I can summon to help me. It rings like an insistent bell, sometimes delicately as a wind chime of translucent shells, sometimes like the bass Marangona of Venice, reverberating through all my thought. And that word is simple—gratitude.

How lucky I am to have lived at the time of the blossoming of all the carefully planted vines, tended by the most extraordinary and varied gardeners. The Library abounded in obsessed personalities in those days: John Archer, a master printer, who turned out such beautiful little booklets from the Library Press, and who was quick to share his knowledge of types and proportion; Romana Javitz, who made the picture morgue of a newspaper office the model for a collection of millions of pictures, serving thousands of artists and agencies in the city (she was always calling us in to see some recent treasure given to the collection); Frances Clarke Sayers, whose meetings were celebrations of the pleasure in books and the people who made them, to name just one of her obsessions; Mr. Thurman, and later Mr. Van Acken, master binders, never too busy to explain an intricate job of mending. Mary Gould Davis, who was in charge of storytelling when I came to the New York Public Library, was a small lady with an absolutely straight back and, somehow, a very jaunty air about her. She often wore an abrupt but smart little leopard coat and a hat with a very long pheasant feather. As soon as she stepped into the doorway, the whole Children's Room was filled with her personality, which seemed so secure. But she told Virginia Mathews, "My dear, you are going to do a great deal of public speaking, and you will be very good. There's no need to be afraid. When I was, I just imagined the audience sitting out there in their underwear, and I was fine."

Some of the most precious exposure we can give the young is to personality—all kinds—often the most precious the most obsessed. As Stendhal wrote, "One can acquire everything in solitude—except character." I am grateful to have worked with librarians like Helen Masten and Maria Cimino, who gave me an idea of what library work with children can be. Helen always saw to it that the whole staff had a chance to meet the fascinating public that came to the old Children's Room on 42nd Street and allowed us to grow as we were able.

As one gets older, gratitude is very easy to feel: gratitude to the eye surgeon, spending day after day in his darkened office, helping hundreds of others to regain the light; gratitude to the therapist who encourages one in the tenacity to rebuild muscles that have atrophied.

196

Edwin Arlington Robinson spoke of "two kinds of gratitude: the sudden kind we feel for what we take, the larger kind we feel for what we give." D'Annunzio's favorite motto was "I have that which I have given."

Gratitude is not always easy to express, especially in any way equal to what one has received—in friendship, in kindness, in love. The audience applauds the lieder singer, who for a time has dispelled the clouds and revealed one little world after another. Perhaps that is why such concerts are so everlastingly refreshing, so completely do they bear us away from our everyday concerns and then, paradoxically, return us to them, renewed, challenged, and delighted, proud to be part of a species that has such experiences of revelation given. All we can do is clap, shout, even "wood it," if the floors are strong enough and we are in some ways young. We would willingly lie down in the mud for the blessed revealer to walk over us dry shod.

How to say thank you for that leap of spirit across space? Perhaps the best and most enduring way, because it ensures a subsequent chain of giving, is passing on to another the revelation and its glow. So the teacher, moved and thrilled, shares the book or the skill. So the librarian, touched by a great spirit, gives through himself or herself of that spirit. And at least one diadem of life is everlasting.

But "love is not love which alters when it alteration finds." Nor does friendship turn away from faults and quirks and bumps in the personality of the friend if it is genuine. Anne Carroll Moore had at least two tremendous advantages, both of which have to do with the extraordinary ability of some people to leave a mark on their time that we like to call genius. She was obsessed, as Frances Sayers put it, "by the knowledge of what excellence in books could mean to chil-

dren." She bent every means at her disposal, including people, to make that obsession effective. She was also born at the
right time and the right place.

I often think of that little girl in Maine, driving through the
snow with her lawyer father to one of his farmer clients, sometimes in "social silence," as she put it, sometimes listening to
stories, memories the road suggested, a child with "the leisure
to grow wise." That girl longed to be a lawyer, but when that
road was closed to her, she took another she was to follow for
the rest of her life. She became one of the gifted young who
converged on the large cities from the forests and wilder-
nesses of the North, the windswept prairies, the small towns
and steamy bogs of the South with their questions—knowing
they would find their own answers.

People who don't or didn't know New York forget that
along with the huge, stimulating mecca, every little section
can have its almost-village type of intimacy. The waves of
migration from Central and Southern Europe brought to New
York people with an injection of color, talent, and a will to
build something new in their lives.

I suppose it was always a bit difficult for those of us who
looked up to others as mentors to realize that we, in turn,
could become mentors to those younger. Friends, if they are
honest, are invaluable in saving one from falling on one's face.
Constantly praising friends are the most dangerous of all. One
had better learn to be deaf to their litanies if one wishes to
grow.

Very often ACM would question her young friends about
some point she wished to write about in her column, especially if her own mind was not quite made up. She could speak
for the young because she listened to them. The other day,
Virginia Mathews and I were exchanging memories of Miss
Moore. We both were young when we knew her as friends.

Virginia—who had an unusual background in children's literature, gained from having read as a child her own mother's extensive and completely preserved childhood library containing all the bound copies of *St. Nicholas* from 1902 on—had been made a buyer of children's books for Brentano's when she was only nineteen. This background enabled her to assess quality in children's books in brilliant reviews in *The New York Times, Virginia Kirkus,* and *Publishers Weekly.*

Miss Moore followed with interest the critical reactions of such people very much younger then herself. *The Three Owls,* standing for author, publisher, and critic, was a critical, ruminative column in *The Horn Book* that often set her pleasure in a book against the background of its timeliness. If there were retractions in judgment to be made, the column was flexible enough to contain second thoughts with grace. But, needless to say, the first judgment had already had its effect on the reception of the book.

I think she would have been appalled at the blurb-quoting, shallow summaries of plots that often pass for reviews today. Even more would she be dismayed to see the simple picture book, a closely knit unit of subject, text, and pictures, so broken down in educational reports into objective categories purporting to have critical importance that they say just about nothing of the book's possible effect on a child's mind. The methods of the New Criticism, carried to the second-grade level, where children are taught to analyze all they read, including the motives of the author for writing it, are terribly old. We almost all grew up stumbling around the edges of Shakespeare, examining the putty on the window frames because no one threw them open and called to us, "Come on in! It's fine here. Here is life!"

I heard of a project to make filmstrips and cassettes, to be used by children, of statements from prize-winning authors and illustrators about the origins of their picture books. I am upset by the trend to get as much educational mileage as possible out of books designed primarily for enjoyment, books that are already crystallizations of what the authors and illustrators wished to communicate to children of their own feeling about a subject. That feeling, whether it is joy, mystery, nonsense, pleasure in personality or whatever, is the message of the book I would want to give the young children for whom most of my books have been done.

I heard of another filmstrip in which the text of *Peter Rabbit* is analyzed, dissected, line by line. Peter is a sturdy little rabbit and has outlived almost a century of imitators, copiers, and sentimental spin-offs. He will keep on being what he was conceived to be, based on the affectionate observation of a live rabbit. But I worry about what may happen to the imaginations of the children in the hands of educators who would seriously undertake such a study. Because surely the next step will be to show some such analysis to children.

There can sometimes be too much attention paid to the persons of the authors and illustrators of children's books, as if some of that individual energy and concentration on an ideal can be transmitted if one listens to words about it. The eternal curiosity about technique can never tell why, where, or even when. Artists of various sorts reinforce the public in its concept of a creator working out of his own psyche, with little thought for his audience, but of course if music is to be played, or a book to be read, or a picture to be seen by others, it is most valuable if it is coherent as communication.

It is often illuminating for us adults to read about the origins of books we love. The creative process is endlessly diverse in details, but, in general, it probably follows a somewhat similar pattern from person to person. Images and sentences appear in a state just under complete consciousness, often when one can't sleep.

Reading is agreeing so wholeheartedly with an author like Emerson when you are a teen-ager and testing your independent mental muscles that you jab your pencil point through the page, so passionately sure you are that he was writing for you. Eudora Welty wrote, "Learning stamps you with its moments. Childhood's learning is made up of moments. It isn't steady. It's a pulse. . . . It had been startling and disappointing to me to find out that story books had been written by *people,* that books were not natural wonders, coming up of themselves, like grass."

Creative people are valuable in whatever field they are. We have no such designation as "National Treasure" in our country for people whose achievements or insights have made them seem indispensable, although there is no dearth of appreciation, even adulation to the point of making some of them cult figures.

On a walk she took one afternoon with John Hyde Preston, Gertrude Stein said, "The thing for the serious writer to remember is that he is writing seriously and is not a salesman. If the writer and the salesman are born in the same man it is lucky for both of them, but if they are not, one is sure to kill the other when you force them together."

It takes a tremendous supply of cockiness—confidence in yourself—to be a writer or an illustrator for children, an honest and tough audience. What makes you think you can do it?

No one knows quite how vulnerable he is to despair if he pauses to question his confidence. Those who write or work creatively themselves are often kinder than those professional ciritics who are brave from a rearguard position. The danger of freezing a person in one phase of his work, of stemming what should be a flood of inventive ideas, is great. I have not looked up the printed record in *The Horn Book* review she wrote, but when I showed Miss Moore my cuts for *Dick Whittington and His Cat,* she was dismayed because I had never been in England, forgetting that the 13th-century settings pertinent to the story no longer existed and that I had the superb resources of the art collections of the New York Public Library and the medieval collections of the Metropolitan Museum of Art for my research. Her lack of confidence taught me the lesson of not showing work in progress, but it also constricted my own faith in myself for months. In a later issue of *The Horn Book,* she reconsidered her first judgment, but the damage had been done.

Why are some people so driven by their desires to paint, write, compose music—or see that children get in their hands the products of people who do? Why are such people never really satisfied with what they do? The job is never done. The book, the picture, never is good enough. If you say so, friends stare at you in disbelief. Aaron Copland had a theory he put forth in one of his Eliot Norton lectures at Harvard: "The reason for the compulsion to renewed creativity is that each added work brings with it an element of self-discovery. I must create in order to know myself, and since self-knowledge is a never-ending search, each new work is only a part answer to the question, 'Who am I?' and brings with it the need to go on to other and different part-answers. All these searchings, unique to those individuals, add up to a compendium of inner experience that eventually tells the world something of itself." An artist cannot will to create a work of art. If it is not spontaneous, it must be cajoled out of innumerable attempts and failures.

I am sure that I speak for many authors and illustrators when I express my gratitude to the librarians and the teachers who have shared our books with children. They have literally kept us and our books alive. The reason most of us never see our books in bookstores is probably caused by the economics of distribution, but it is distressing to the authors and maddening for their friends.

Newness should not be pursued for itself. That is surely the way to triteness and a speedy fall out of fashion. But a slow, developing familiarity with material will eventually cause it to show that it is *itself* and needs its own treatment. Much as Miss Moore admired the work of creative people—but "admired" is too tame a word for her concentrated delight—I often felt that she did not seem to understand much of the creative inspiration of others, or simply how people work. "Five years is necessary to make a good picture book," she would announce, with a cavalier disregard for my economics. I could have told her, "More. You need a whole lifetime."

When Miss Moore was influencing the publishing of books she wished to see in the hands of children, we were seeing the first publicity and promotion departments in the children's book field. Young, energetic, and attractive people with unlimited enthusiasm for the books on a publisher's list and an ability to give stirring book talks that created a hunger for those books traveled around the country. Appearances by authors were occasional and special. Today, so often the authors travel around the country, speaking at workshops that may be part of a package that will be publishable proof that the professor is worthy of tenure or recognition by his university. I often wonder how many books never get written because of this loss of concentration and energy.

It seems odd, but the arbitrary limit of time to what we call a century is often a time of summing up and of extraordinary change. Our little boats are already rocking in a new wind. Some of the vines are torn now and ravaged; some have stuck their heads in the earth and instead of hiding, seem to grow just as well upside down. Vital juices can run in both directions, it seems, and even the feet can spring into flowers, as poets have known for years.

We can't go home again, turn back time, or even hold it in suspension. If we needed to learn the tragedy of standing still in time, Natalie Babbitt's *Tuck Everlasting* would teach us. Miss Moore's time was and is not the present time, although in a way it is.

In a letter to Van Wyck Brooks, Lewis Mumford wrote, "Now war is as grim as the assembly line of a Ford factory and as relentless as a financier: the morals of the rattlesnake are everywhere. . . . When we were young we could ask ourselves: What can we conquer? Now we can only ask: What can we save?" That was in 1936. In 1984 seemingly crazed world leaders are thinking so irresponsibly about human life and resources that it might be appropriate to put them, while still living, in a zoo: "This mutant, once called Man, is now a monster."

In their dedication, commitment, involvement—call it what you will—there are some people whose whole beings are more closely identified with what they do than others. When at last such a person retires from public life and work, if he does not have a new beginning, the experience can be traumatic and difficult for all concerned. One must step aside for the next in line to have his chance in his own way to work out his own fulfillment. Once Miss Moore said to me, "But you are never lonely, are you?" and revealed a poignant truth about herself, when she could no longer function as she had. There was in her remark also a wistfulness for the kind of creativity she knew was not hers.

"Human friendship, at its deepest level, is perhaps the most important factor in our lives. It is the one relationship which keeps a space between people; what is given in friendship is always a bonus because no one owes anybody anything, or wants anything, there are no duties involved; one is quite free." So Janet Baker writes in *Full Circle.* "Performers come and go. The music is what matters. The music is for always."

The delicately humorous and rueful acceptance of being unrequited in love can be transformed by Mozart into a modest violet, almost happy to be trod on and used by the heedless loved one. "It was a gracious violet."

Gratitude: the older to the younger spins a web of bonds. When I was in high school, I had read about Povlah Frisch, the great Danish lieder singer. My small study in the parsonage on Wurts Street in Kingston, New York, just big enough to hold an old desk my father had given me, a chair, and a bookcase, had its walls papered with Lawrence Gilman's music criticisms from *The New York Herald Tribune.* Among them were descriptions of Povlah Frisch's unforgettable lieder recitals in Town Hall. When I later became part of the Children's Room staff in New York, I was accustomed to modest dreams, perforce, about what I would get a chance to hear and see in New York, since I earned little. Can you imagine—but you can't—my pleasure when Maria Cimino invited me to hear Povlah Frisch in Town Hall? Some of the little worlds she revealed—the mystery of walking in velvet shoes, the snow, in Randall Thompson's setting of Elinor Wylie's lovely poem; the René Clair boredom of Francis Poulenc's French children on their Sunday promenade; the rapturous images of deLisle and Fauré's "Nell." I never forgot that concert. Some years later, on the celebration of Hans Christian Andersen's birthday, again I heard Povlah Frisch, in her telling of "The Story of a Mother," chilling, terrifying, and intense as a Kollwitz print.

Maria Cimino and I shared many talks about music as often we literally climbed around the tops of the bookcases, arranging the beautiful exhibitions that were part of Maria's song. Through gratitude, one forms one's own ideals.

My first summer storytelling, under Mary Gould Davis, I traveled all over the city with my stories and bag of never-fail picture books to the playgrounds, day camps, on the book-mobiles. I had as example the frank gusto of Miss Davis, who felt her stories so that the children felt them too. At St. John's Villa Academy on Staten Island, one hot July afternoon, a group of children seemed exactly ready for "The White Horse Girl and the Blue Wind Boy" of Carl Sandburg, one of my favorites. And then there was another group at 67th Street, with concentrated little Chinese faces, tears streaming down their cheeks because of Rapunzel's blindness.

Can we ever be grateful enough to the children, sighing with effort as they stood on a chair, writing their names on the applications to get their first library cards? The intense ones, like Anna Fuss, recently a refugee from Germany, who every Saturday walked from the eighties because it was her Sabbath and who was already a leader in her class. I often wonder to what Anna later applied that passionate intensity.

Throughout my career the memory of those children and their reactions have been personal traffic controls for my work: *Stop, steep grade, slippery when wet, yield,* and *a light ahead.*

I am at an age when some of the letters that are precious to me come from adults who read my books as children and are trying to locate them again. Some color, some bower of their own imagining, constructed with a residue of images left from the book, they wish to recapture, to reenter, to share with their own children. Aida Metzenberg from Wisconsin: "My very favorite picture book eluded me. I remembered it as full of warm, bright, and colorful pictures of exotic princes and a princess, and I remembered the story, but I remembered the

206

title as *The Magic Carpet,* which was unfortunately incorrect. . . . Then I tried to think of another book I liked as well and all I could think of was *Stone Soup.*"

I would like to share with you parts of a letter that was handed to me as I was about to speak in Iowa City some years ago. It was from a librarian and storyteller, Bonnie West, now married to an artist. Some of you will remember her as Emily Mazur, who, with her mother and sisters, made the long trek from the upper Bronx to 42nd Street on Saturday afternoons. She writes: "It was the highlight of our days. It created a pattern of life for me—that of looking to the library as a source of pleasure and excitement on a continuing basis. . . . I remember, for instance, the anticipation with which we walked through the marble corridors of the 42nd Street Library . . . and how the lucky first-in-line child was allowed to knock ceremoniously on the heavy wooden door, and how the ornate handle would slowly, mysteriously turn, and how the door would open from the inside, revealing the storyteller for the day, who would greet us in muted tones. And how the only light was candlelight, and how we sat on low stools in a semicircle around the storyteller, in an atmosphere that made me, for one, feel as though I were in the middle of a story. The images evoked were so real to me. And I remember, particularly, the precise language and cultured tones of the storytellers' voices (which were so much in contrast with the speech patterns and intonations which surrounded us in the New York streets and schools). . . . Of all the librarians who told stories, I remember you and Maria Cimino most vividly. . . . You almost created music in the storytelling. . . . I would have given anything to have been able to expose my own children to such beautifully planned, image-laden story hours. And I remember Helen Masten suggesting that since I loved the Laura Ingalls Wilder books much, I should write and tell her so. You can't imagine the thrill it was to get, as a result, a return letter from Mrs. Wilder herself. And I remember getting a telegram (because we didn't have a telephone) from the librarian at the 42nd Street library, inviting us to a prepublishing reading of the "Grandfather Tales" by Richard Chase. . . . It's hard to reduce to words the images one retains from childhood. I wish more children could have the 'magical' experiences I feel I had at the library when I was a child. . . . I consider libraries to be among the most important institutions in our culture. Enough. . . . "

Gratitude: I think of the young teachers and former librarians who are starting quality bookstores for children, such as The Story Hour in Honolulu or Pinocchio in Pittsburgh, where children can find a wealth of good books, not only the newest or the most commercial. I think of the teachers of teachers and librarians, as I have met them across the country, who have maintained a freshness in their appraisal of the needs of children—Mae Durham Roger, John Rowell, Shelton Root, Jane Bingham, Pat Scales, Mildred Laughlin. There are many more—all pivots. And in South Carolina, now, there is Augusta Baker, active in her workshops, encouraging and inspiring young teachers and librarians, and us, and telling stories better than ever. I think of the librarians I have been grateful to meet as they stood in long lines at conventions to take back stacks of books to their libraries—a bouncing young librarian from New Jersey, thrilled to be in Alaska, where everything seemed to her "new." I think of Momoko Ishii, who came to know Anne Carroll Moore in New York and went back to introduce the picture books she had known and loved here to Japanese children and publishers. I think of the young librarian I met from the Seminole country of Florida, teaching old people from a trailer camp nearby to read in her children's room because they had had to work in the fields as children and never had a chance to learn.

Once more, I quote Janet Baker in her book *Full Circle,* because she writes as she sings, directly and from the "heart of the matter," with no affectation: "Can I claim, as a woman, to feel completely fulfilled? There are innumerable ways for human beings to 'give birth.' You do not have to be female but you do have to be a channel for life. . . . Our work can give birth to change, can touch, heal, comfort, or bring joy to the human heart. . . . This power is not a prerogative of artists; anyone can discover it in any simple act made by one person to another in the course of daily life. . . . Artists are wielding this power at any one moment to large numbers of people. In ordinary life the numbers are smaller, but the process is exactly the same, and so is the end result—fulfillment."

The last time I saw Anne Carroll Moore was in the Christmas season. She had been ill with a kind of flu that was close to pneumonia and was very weak. There was no energy at all for words; so we didn't talk. She grasped my hand and just smiled gently at me. After a few minutes she lit one of the little wish- ing candles always ready. We both just sat there, warmed by the tiny light, in silence. No one blew out the candle this time. We both knew it was good-bye. The bird-bone lightness as we embraced. . . .

Bundled up in blankets, she took a last excursion in the city she adored. Alexandra Sanford took her in a big Checker cab on one more ride in what was to her the city of light—New York at Christmas season: the great tree at Rockefeller Center, Macy's, Altman's, Lord and Taylor. The windows of the big department stores celebrated family warmth, fairy tales, a childlike kind of fantasy. A short time afterwards, she died.

A few weeks after her death, a memorial service was held

in the church she loved, across Fifth Avenue from the Grosvenor—the Ascension. Afterwards, those who had come to remember and honor her were invited by Storer Lunt to the Grosvenor for the kind of party she would have given. Time was whizzing around us all that day, diving back fifty years for some, leaping ahead for others. It was the kind of party where friends gazed into each other's eyes and smiled and embraced, with no need to speak. But of course there was speaking, and laughter, and the mellowness of affectionate and grateful memory. The large room was filled with the editors and librarians she had worked with, the authors and artists whose work she had delighted in. Having recently returned from Italy, I found myself chatting to Pamela Bianco in the language of her childhood in Italy, when her exquisite drawings had first entranced Miss Moore. Bringing together people whose joy it had been to work for children in the best way they could had been one of her favorite ways of celebration.

At one point, Fred Melcher came up to me, his face radiant. He smiled and said quietly, "Marcia, there's something in the air. . . . " There was indeed. There is.

INDEX

Brown, Marcia: on Africa, 169-73, 179-80, 184-85; on Anne Carroll Moore, 193-95, 197-99, 202-03, 204, 208-10; approach to work, 68-74, 152-53, 203, 204; in Bali, Indonesia, 99-102; on betrayal, 147-48, 153-58; and the Caldecott Medal, 177-78; childhood influences on, 19-21, 30; in Denmark, 95, 96-98; goals as an illustrator, 61-62; on gratitude, 196-98, 202, 205, 208; in Hawaii, 53, 72; on lotus seeds, 150-51, 158-59; in New York Public Library, 79, 163-64, 179, 206-08; playing the flute, 133-34; and the Regina Medal, 135-37; on *Shadow*, 164, 167-69, 171-73, 177-89; and *The Snow Queen*, 93; studying under Judson Smith, 154-55; teaching English, 45; use of photography, 87, 96; on value of history, 173; in Virgin Islands, 28; and *The Wild Swans*, 71-72; work on *Once a Mouse . . .*, 35-37; work with woodcuts, 73, 93, 94-95

Bryson, Bernarda, 108
Buddha, 141-42
Burch, Robert, 51

Caldecott Medal, 86, 177
Caldecott, Randolph, 9, 19
Calico Bush, 64
Campbell, Joseph, 137, 184, 188
Carigiet, Alois, 125
Carrick, Donald, 89
Cather, Willa, 94
The Cat Who Went to Heaven, 136
Cendrars, Blaise (Frederic-Louis Sauser), 164, 167-69, 177, 179-80, 184, 185
Chan, Plato, 6
Characterization in picture books, 11, 157
Charlip, Remy, 117
Charlot, Jean, 136
Chase, Richard, 208
Chermayeff, Ivan, 117
Childhood: art in, 25; artists' integrity toward, 103-04; betrayal of, 147-49, 151-53, 155, 157; effects

of books in, 46-49, 50-53, 55, 103-04; the heritage of, 31; intuitive mind of, 54-55, 166-67, 168-69, 180; need for heroes, 47-49, 55-56, 139-40; poetic mind of, 183; push into precocity and, 135; and stereotypes, 187; and story identification, 21-22; symbolism in color, 27; training visual awareness in, 4, 6-7, 12, 13; and value of history, 173

Children's Book Council, 86
Children's Book Showcase, 86
A Child's Christmas in Wales, 117
A Child's Good Night Book, 7
Ching-Li and the Dragon, 136
Cimino, Maria, 164, 179, 196, 205, 207
Cinderella, 31, 69
Clair, Rene, 89, 205
Clean Peter and the Children of Grubbylea, 20
Cole, William, 125
Colette, 49
Collage, 67, 88-89, 120-22
Color: meanings, 24, 27-28; in picture books, 6-8, 10-11, 122-23
Colum, Padraic, 136
Cooney, Barbara, 125
Cooper, James Fenimore, 20
Copland, Aaron, 202
The Coronation of Poppaea, 164
Creative Intuition in Art and Poetry, 22
Creative process: clear exposition of, 22-24; illusiveness of, 68, 200; and metaphor, 165; time required for, 203-04; transcendence of story in, 56-57, 62
Criticism, 65, 112; and "New Criticism," 199-200; personality of critics in, 166, 185-86; vulnerability to, 201-02
Cruikshank, 68, 124

Dai Nippon, 177
Dalgliesh, Alice, 24; childhood of, 81; in Connecticut, 79-81; as editor, 29, 79; in New York Public Library, 79
Dance, 169